# Environmental Scanning
## *for* Associations

The Everyday Guide to
Capturing, Analyzing, and Interpreting
Strategic Information

JAMES DALTON

AND

ALAN BALKEMA

**asae**
association
management
press

WASHINGTON, DC

The authors have worked diligently to ensure that all information in this book is accurate as of the time of publication and consistent with standards of good practice in the general management community. As research and practice advance, however, standards may change. For this reason it is recommended that readers evaluate the applicability of any recommendations in light of particular situations and changing standards.

ASAE: The Center for Association Leadership
Association Management Press
1575 I Street, NW
Washington, DC 20005-1103
Phone: (202) 626-2723; (888) 950-2723 outside the metropolitan Washington, DC area
Fax: (202) 220-6439
Email: books@asaecenter.org
We connect great ideas and great people to inspire leadership and achievement in the association community.

Keith C. Skillman, CAE, Vice President, Publications,
    ASAE: The Center for Association Leadership
Baron Williams, CAE, Director of Book Publishing,
    ASAE: The Center for Association Leadership

Cover design by Beth Lower, ASAE: The Center for Association Leadership
Interior design by Troy Scott Parker, Cimarron Design, cimarrondesign.com

This book is available at a special discount when ordered in bulk quantities. For information, contact the ASAE Member Service Center at (202) 371-0940.

A complete catalog of titles is available on the ASAE website at www.asaecenter.org.

ISBN-13: 978-0-88034-347-3
ISBN-10: 0-88034-347-8

Printed in the United States of America.

10 9 8 7 6 5 4 3 2 1

# Contents

Preface   v

CHAPTER 1
What Is Environmental Scanning?   1

CHAPTER 2
Achieving a Common Understanding   11

CHAPTER 3
Designing and Implementing an Environmental Scanning
Process   23

CHAPTER 4
Getting Started   37

CHAPTER 5
Strategy Management   49

## Case Studies
1 *A New Scan Plan*   65
2 *Tracking Trends*   68
3 *And the Survey Says...*   71
4 *All Together Now: Scanning and Strategic Planning*   75
5 *Asked and Answered*   79
6 *Extra! Extra! Read All About It*   82
7 *Staff-Driven Scanning*   85

## Appendices
1 *Mapping Your Personal Future*   91
2 *Template for Reporting on a Trend or Issue*   93

About the Authors   95

# Preface

In anticipation of an update on environmental scanning the ASAE Foundation conducted a mini-survey of a sample of ASAE's membership in fall 2010, which asked four yes-no questions about their environmental scanning activities and an open-ended question about which association is "good" at environmental scanning.

Subsequently, the authors telephoned a range of mini-survey respondents and asked them to explain their scanning activities in more detail. Those associations that were identified multiple times on the "good" question were also contacted to learn more about their process. A selection of interviews from six different associations and trade groups outlining their scanning processes and experiences appears later in this book. The authors also conducted secondary research and drew on their own expertise to inform the writing of this guidebook.

One common element of the telephone interviews was that the association executive was often responsible for adapting a hit-and-miss, board-meeting-driven approach to issues' consideration into a well-defined, carefully thought-out process.

For example, after her participation in the healthcare industry town hall meeting held as part of ASAE's *Defining Your Future* process, Oncology Nursing Society executive director for external relations and business development Michelle Dietz realized that change was occurring too fast for her organization's old process to be effective. She began work to adapt ONS's strategic process from a once-every-three-years look at potential issues that informed the organization's decisions to an ongoing process that involved all staff.

Throughout this book, we will highlight other association executives' journeys with scanning and the processes that we learned about during their interviews.

Environmental scanning should be a nimble process, well-defined but adaptable to change and focused on a goal of identifying the trends that may affect your association. It also demonstrates that the collection of information is followed by a process where this information is put to the test through discussion, debate, and feedback before trends are adopted.

To be proactive, however, an association must also take the time to prepare for the trends it accepts as being a probable influence or actor on the association. What good is accepting that a trend is probably coming if you don't assess how that trend will affect your association and what you can do in advance to mitigate the impact or best take advantage of the opportunity?

Environmental scanning is not a board meeting agenda item, but a journey undertaken by an association to achieve a sustainable future. This book is a guide for association executives and other leaders to use in structuring and executing their organizations' environmental scanning activities. We encourage association executives to use this book to move forward with their own journeys.

In addition to this guidebook, the ASAE Foundation maintains trends available on the ASAE website at www.asaecenter.org/spi/sia.cfm, where you can also find ASAE's Scan to Plan Interactive Tool for prioritizing trends that may affect your organization. The foundation conducts a Delphi process to identify new trends or reconfirm existing trends that will affect associations, as well as weak signals of change appearing on the horizon, to broaden and deepen association executives' thinking about strategic options. The foundation conducts the Delphi process semi-annually to keep 50 key trends up to date.

Using the STEEP (Social, Technology, Economy, Environment, Political) framework, a librarian conducts a search of databases and meta-scanning sites to identify potential new trends. The librarian uses keywords identified in *Designing Your Future*'s "100 Emerging Trends" within the STEEP categories.

Emerging trends are combined with the existing trends for the purpose of the ranking. Members of the ASAE Foundation Research Committee and ad hoc ASAE volunteers receive an email outlining the objectives of the study, a schedule for response, a short description of trends, and the questionnaire. The respondents perform the following duties

- Rate the trends on Likert scales according to likely impact on and importance to associations.
- Comment on the trends as appropriate.
- Identify additional trends that should be considered.

The first-round response is analyzed and the feedback synthesized. The rankings on the first round determine the order of the list of trends to be ranked in the second round. Respondents again assess the trends on the same Likert scales with another opportunity to comment and add additional trends. If no broad consensus emerges on the 50 key trends after the second round, a third round is undertaken.

The ASAE Foundation uses this method to keep the 50 key trends appearing on the website relevant to the association world.

# CHAPTER 1

# What Is Environmental Scanning?

Environmental scanning is the means by which an organization observes the changing conditions around it and then incorporates this information into carefully crafted adaptations aimed at ensuring future viability. In rapidly changing environments, one rule of thumb applies: *If you don't adapt, you don't endure.*

Environmental scanning is sometimes dismissed as being little more than monitoring news sources and writing reports on the activity. It is true that any scanning process includes these two elements, but the activity directly attributable to the distinct value scanning offers lies in between monitoring and reporting.

Environmental scanning is a collaborative sense-making process. When done well, it draws a community of interests into a thoughtful discussion about how the environment is changing and what that means for the future. This process shouldn't be delegated to a small group of people, because the real value is found in the sense-making process itself, not the report that gets generated as a result of it. Making sense of changing conditions requires cognitive abilities that include a heightened awareness of what is going on around you, which couples with the ability to discern the parts of that panoply that will make big differences in the long run.

This requires a community of interests for two reasons. First, the more people you have involved, the more inputs and cognitive processing capacity you have. It's like a big information technology system that really gets cranking. More importantly, the people involved in the process not only produce insights on the future, they absorb them. Second, they take heightened awareness and sharpened discernment home with them where they apply them to recognizing prospects for their careers, families, and businesses.

A considerable body of knowledge has developed on environmental scanning, but it's heavily oriented toward for-profit organizations and doesn't fully recognize the organizational nature and unique conditions of associations. To address this, for nearly two decades, ASAE has provided a series of scanning resources that translate this knowledge into an association context while trying to capture what can be learned from the scanning experiences of associations (See sidebar).

## Guidebook's Purpose

The purpose of this guidebook is to capitalize on these resources and focus on three primary objectives:

- Present a framework that explains the basic elements of a scanning process for associations.

- Explain the fundamental concepts that are critical to success when establishing a scanning process.

- Provide illustrations and tools from associations that are scanning and reference other scanning resources that are available from ASAE.

## A Scanning Framework

There are an endless number of variations in the way associations go about environmental scanning, but all of them can be accounted for within a seven-step framework of basic elements that should be addressed in any situation. This guidebook is designed around this basic framework for environmental scanning.

1. **Achieve a common understanding of the term *scanning* and your environment.**
   A straightforward definition of scanning was given in the opening of this chapter. Unfortunately, not everyone shares a common understanding of what scanning involves, not even

the business scholars who write about it. So the first order of business is to consider the implications and agree on a common understanding that best suits the needs of your association. Chapter 2 provides several definitions from recognized authorities on the subject and highlights the differences.

Next you need to clarify what will be included in your use of the term *environment* and that gets more complicated. To begin with, every association has two environments to consider: the immediate and the universal. The first includes the community of related interests and affected parties. For an industry association, this includes suppliers, competitors, distributors, and customers. For professional associations, it involves enablers such as educators and employers, related professions, support personnel, and customers. In the business literature, this is referred to as the task environment.

The universal environment is the rest of the world where major trends are brewing up significant implications for every industry and profession. It's a much bigger environment to account for, and scanning it requires more resources and higher tolerance for abstraction. For example, the way we teach elementary school children today is very different from the education today's business executives experienced. The implications from this will affect the next generation's career choices, work habits, and workplace expectations. Ideally, both environments should be addressed, but limited resources and a sense of urgency to address immediate issues makes the task environment the typical starting point. However this sorts out, people should understand the parameters.

Within the task environment, there are other factors that should be considered in arriving at a common understanding of your environment's unique characteristics. This analysis will define the type of challenges you are facing and the resources you will need to do a competent job. If this analysis is not done well, different people will have different expectations of the scanning process and that spells trouble. Chapter 2 identifies these considerations and describes how they apply to associations.

## 2. Establish a team.

Scanning isn't for everyone. Some people have a greater appetite for thinking about the future than others. There are differences in the types of contributions staff and volunteers are positioned to make. The number of people required for a scanning process will also vary according to the environmental conditions.

## 3. Identify sources and assign responsibilities.

Like environments, sources can be grouped into two types. Regular sources are predictable, consistent information sources that relate directly to your industry or profession. This might include everything from *The New York Times* to industry journals and blogs. Irregular sources are those identified through the serendipity of searching without much of a plan and always being ready to recognize relevant information anywhere you may find it.

## 4. Compare, evaluate, and format.

Scanned information, when first encountered and captured, is extremely disparate. It could be fact or conjecture, present or future, peer-reviewed science, or internet scuttlebutt. Initially, it can be captured in some raw form, such as a short paragraph and a reference. However, if it is thought to be relevant, this information should be refined into a consistent format that facilitates comparing, tagging, storing, and retrieving.

There is a difference between a "trend" that may affect many industries and professions in unspecified ways and an "issue" that refines a trend into an assertion on how a trend will affect the association's community. All of this requires developing operational definitions for key terms and a process for connecting disparate bits of information and referencing refined batches, such as credible reports.

## 5. Vet the findings.

Recognizing bits of relevant information can be demanding, but interpreting them to determine how they might affect the association's constituents is much more difficult. Chapter 3 describes a vetting process that lets the scanning team members postulate an effect of a particular trend on a specific segment of their organization's members and then test their thinking through encounters with those constituents.

Anywhere, anytime members are or can be gathered is an opportunity for some vetting. Not only does this improve the predicted effect, it strengthens the political credibility. The leadership of an association can dismiss an issue presented to them by an internal scanning team, but it is far less apt to be dismissed if successive member groups acknowledge and stand behind it.

## 6. Develop useful scanning outputs.

So what do you do with a scanning report when this long process brings important trends to light? Common practice has one answer to that question. Give it to the strategic planning committee for its work in developing adaptations—a.k.a. strategies—to help keep the organization up on changing conditions. Chapters 4 and 5 take the position that the format of the scanning report for this purpose must be one that directly connects with whatever process is in place to develop these strategies. Otherwise, a general prose document on the environment may be viewed as just another burdensome document to read before the next committee meeting.

There is a second potential output for scanning that is gaining popularity for associations. If the members are involved in strategic planning for their organizations, they might find the association's environmental scan to be of enormous value. While this will probably require different formatting, the scanning report could have value as a revenue-producing resource for the association.

## 7. Keep it going.

Many associations that do scan in an organized manner do so on a periodic basis, like once every three years as a precursor to the periodic strategic planning process. Those who see value in multiple outputs like an annual scanning publication or a feeder to scanning sessions at the annual meeting realize that scanning should be an established, ongoing process.

As is apparent in this framework, environmental scanning should be a nimble process, well-defined but adaptable to change and focused on a goal of identifying the trends that may affect your association. It also demonstrates that the collection of information is followed by a process where this information is put to the test through discussion, debate, and feedback, before trends are adopted.

To be proactive, however, an association must also take the time to prepare for the trends it accepts as being a probable influence or actor on the association. What good is accepting that a trend is probably coming if you don't assess how that trend will impact your association and what you can do in advance to mitigate the impact or best take advantage of the opportunity?

Environmental scanning is not an occasional activity. Instead, it is an ongoing effort by an association to monitor trends towards achieving a sustainable future. This book is a roadmap for association executives and other leaders to use in organizing and implementing their organizations' environmental scanning activities.

## A Unique Role for Associations

The body of literature on scanning includes a growing number of references to nonprofit organizations, but very few to associations per se. This is unfortunate because there is a unique, uncelebrated role for associations in the field of environmental scanning. The association industry's failure to appreciate this is not surprising given the way it failed to capitalize on unique capabilities in areas such as networking. Associations have always known they were an excellent venue for networking and most include this claim in their marketing pitches. However, when you ask association executives about their budgets for networking or the name of the staff person in charge of it, they are apt to give you a strange look. The implication one might draw from this is alarming. It's as if they were saying: *"Networking is important, but it's a byproduct of what we do. We offer meetings and if you come then networking happens."* Many associations woke up to this embarrassing point only after the business literature started writing books on how important networking is to knowledge workers. If networking is so valuable, maybe it should be elevated from a byproduct to a program with resources and performance metrics to make sure it meets customer expectations.

This correlates with the notion that environmental scanning is something you do simply as input to the strategic planning process. Every profession and industry is scrambling to figure out how their environments are changing in ways that affect what they do. They all feel pressure from accelerating rates of change. They're networking to find out what their peers think about changing conditions. So here's a thought. Perhaps environmental scanning should be thought of as a value proposition for the members to help them figure out how they need to adapt. Input to the association's strategic plan might be the byproduct.

This notion is directly connected to the networking function and more importantly to the concern many association executives have over the prospect of the internet allowing easy access to other networking venues, thereby depreciating the value offered by the association. This is a legitimate concern if networking is thought of simply as an exchange of information and an opportunity to develop contacts. A distinguishing feature of an association is the ability to extract information from these networks, add some research and analysis, and provide a whole new information-based product. Environmental scanning is greatly enhanced by the number of people who offer their insights. This makes networking and environmental scanning siblings that associations are uniquely positioned to combine and capitalize on. The enhanced value proposition might read: *Networking to share ideas, make valuable contacts, and gain insight on the how the future will affect you.*

## The Changing Nature of Planning

From its origins in the 60s, strategic planning evolved into a fairly standard process that came into play for a brief period. The purpose was to produce a plan that described the adaptations that should take place during a subsequent time period. Planning then went dormant until this cycle was repeated. The two key concepts here are "periodic" and a "plan." By the turn of the millennium, business leaders started taking issue with this strategic planning template, and their criticism focused on these two attributes. Rates of change had accelerated to a point where they thought adaptations should be conceived and managed in an ongoing process. Furthermore, they thought the idea of a "plan" implied a fixed document that held sway for an extended period. Chapter 5 elaborates on a new planning framework where the term *strategic planning* is replaced by *strategy management*. The change is intended to convey an ongoing governing function where the dynamic concept of a strategy is the focal point, not a document.

When strategic planning happened once every two or three years, a scan that went beyond a SWOT session on a given day was rare. There were no standard formats for scanning or scanning documents as there were for strategic planning. Consequently, association scans from that time for which there are any records tended to be loosely structured prose documents that might be characterized as "observations on things." There were no operational definitions to provide meaningful structure or utilities to produce findings that had fitness for use.

An ongoing strategy management process means every time a board meets there are two distinctly different governing sessions. The first is a management session where budgets are approved, people are nominated, and committee reports are considered. Then, there is a strategic session where only two things are considered: 1) how the environment is changing and 2) what is being done to adapt. This kind of governance requires a steady stream of reliable information on changing conditions.

## The ASAE Foundation's Scanning Activities

Since its first environmental scan in 1995, the ASAE Foundation has continued to develop the craft of environmental scanning in the association world. Here's an overview of its key scanning activities, which began with a survey of a sample of ASAE membership on the topic of information technology and resulted in the convening of trend analysis panels to explore the implications of the information technology explosion.

Two years later, the foundation held a New Horizons Think Tank, a high-level forum of leaders from inside and outside the association industry that explored ways to get beyond incremental thinking about the future.

In the foundation's 1998 environmental scan, technology experts assessed technology's promise for associations and identified macro trends. Representatives from associations, convention and visitor bureaus, the hospitality industry, and consulting firms then whittled those down to the specific trends and issues most relevant to the association community.

Two ASAE publications chronicled these large undertakings: *Facing the Future* and *Embracing the Future,* both published in 1999.

To look further out into the planning horizon, the foundation formed a virtual community to conduct a dialogue about scanning. Participants in the virtual community included association executives, futurists, and guest experts. Issues identified in this online discussion were evaluated in a series of focus groups with association leaders, business partners, and consultants and through literature reviews. The ASAE publication *Exploring the Future* (2001) reported on these activities and the trends that emerged.

In 2005 and 2006, the foundation sponsored a series of focus groups and surveys that identified eight "super-trends" influencing every sector of an association's business. These activities were reported in the ASAE publication *Mapping the Future of Your Association* (2005–2006).

The foundation launched the *Association of the Future* program in 2007. A lengthy environmental scan resulted in 50 key trends considered important to the association community, which were profiled in the ASAE publication *Designing Your Future* (2008). These 50 key trends were listed on the ASAE foundation website and continue to be updated.

## Leadership Implications

The information provided by an ongoing environmental scanning process can have a very positive effect on the experience of serving on a board. Board meetings that include credible research about how the industry or professional environment is changing are something that appeals to industry leaders. These days, top industry leaders are hard pressed to take an active role in an association unless they can justify it within the context of their business obligations. If the assignment is more about leading the industry than it is about overseeing an association, it takes on much greater appeal. Quality environmental scanning is a critical ingredient in developing that impression and meeting the expectations it creates.

In a strategic planning session for an association, you will frequently hear some say: *"Wait a minute, are we doing a strategic plan for the association or for the industry/profession?"* This confusion is a positive sign that makes an important point. Members don't pay dues so the association can improve its business prospects. They pay dues so the association can improve the collective interests of the businesses or professionals it represents. The association is a means to that end, and the planning process must account for the distinction. However, if the focus is on a community's prosperity, it is a leadership value proposition, not an administrative task.

Now that we've established a framework for environmental scanning and discussed the unique role for associations in the process, the next chapter will highlight the importance of establishing a common lexicon and shared goals before your association begins scanning.

CHAPTER 2

# Achieving a Common Understanding

This chapter addresses the terms and conceptual framework of environmental scanning. The purpose is twofold: 1) to help you make sure everyone involved has a common understanding of what scanning is and what to expect from it and 2) to help you analyze the type of environment you are scanning. In other words, it's about the areas you need to understand and clarify before you start scanning.

## Systems Theory and Environmental Scanning

Chapter 1 mentioned that some people think environmental scanning simply may amplify a leader's awareness of what's going on in the world, but at the risk of turning what should be a simple research assignment into an ongoing process. To understand the fundamental importance of environmental scanning in today's world, the field of systems theory gives some insights that might be useful in achieving a common understanding. At first this discussion may seem a little too theoretical or abstract, but it does have a practical purpose.

Three interwoven terms from systems theory give context to help understand what occurs when organizations engage in environmental scanning:

- An **environment** is the array of circumstances and conditions that surround any given system, be it a pollywog in a pond or an organization in a marketplace.

- A **system** is an interdependent collection of processes bound together by a common purpose. A system is critically dependent upon some but not all of the environmental conditions surrounding it.

- A **process** is a repeating set of procedures that come together in a way that transforms certain types of inputs into value-added outputs.

An association is a **system** that incorporates a variety of **processes** like publishing, educating, and advocating. An advocacy process, for example, receives inputs like news of emerging legislation that may affect the members, and it produces outputs like positions and strategies that are intended to affect the legislation. The issues are always changing, but the procedures established to recognize, analyze, and strategize around them all come together in a predictable manner that gets repeated for each new issue. In systems theory, this is a process. (In association terms, these processes are called programs, but let's stick with systems-speak for just a little bit.)

A **system** is thought to be viable when its **processes** are stable, which means they operate efficiently, effectively, and predictably. Once a system achieves this state of stability, everything would be wonderful from then on but for one disruptive fact. The conditions surrounding the system are always changing. Most of these changes are incidental, and the system blows them off. However, the system is critically dependent on some of the conditions, and when they change, the system enters a critical intersection: either adapt in a manner that accommodates the change and strengthens the system or drift into extinction.

For the system to adapt and remain viable, some of the processes must be redesigned or jettisoned altogether so that resources can move into new processes. In nature, systems throw off random mutations that serendipitously match up with changing conditions and that good fortune assures their future viability. In human systems, the cognitive ability to know when the environment is changing in a way that warrants thoughtful adaptation is a competency that's increasingly important as the rate of change accelerates.

Discussing systems theory helps make the point that environmental scanning is not a fad nor is it mere awareness on steroids. It is a fundamental survival capacity, and it is critical to a system's viability. When change occurred at a comfortable pace, which it once did, leaving it to the awareness of leaders may have been adequate, but the pace of environmental change has accelerated to a point where general awareness won't cut it. Improving the discipline, rigor, and productivity of your system's awareness capacity improves its viability and position in the ecosystem.

## Definitions

The term *environmental scanning* contains several distinct elements. Unfortunately, there is no universally accepted definition that brings them all together. The first scholar to study scanning was F.J. Aguilar (1967) and he defined it as *"the way in which management gathers relevant information about events occurring outside the company in order to guide the company's future course of action."* With a subtle but significantly different perspective, J. David Hunger and Thomas L. Wheelen (2000) said, *"The purpose of environmental scanning is to identify strategic factors, external and internal elements that will determine the future of the corporation."*

The most apparent difference between these definitions is that the first says scanning is about events outside the organization while the second includes elements that are both "external and internal." In strategic planning language, that suggests a full SWOT analysis where the objective is to identify the organization's strengths, weaknesses, opportunities, and threats. Aguilar implies something less than that. His approach is more of an OT analysis since opportunities and threats are typically external to the organization. If you are asked to do a scan, this is an important distinction to make. Are you looking strictly at the environment outside the organization, or are you including an internal organizational assessment? Most of the experts probably agree with the external-only definition but getting everyone to agree on this either way is important.

A second difference in these definitions is far more subtle. The first one makes a straightforward connection between gathering environmental information and guiding future actions as if environmental scanning and strategic planning should be thought of as one seamlessly connected operation. The second definition emphasizes the task of identifying strategic factors that will have impact on the future of the organization, but it makes no reference to the activity that determines those actions. So what's the big deal?

In the context of association management, there's a pair of big deals. First, strategic planning and environmental scanning operate on different frequencies and require different skill sets. Scanning should be continuous, like radar. It's always on, sifting through a lot of information, culling out observations that may be relevant to the organization's future. A case can be made that strategic planning should also be constant, or at least ongoing, but for most organizations it is a periodic process at best, and unfortunately, thought of as something only very important people do, and their time is dear. Scanning requires patience, a certain tolerance for abstraction, and a willingness to explore wide spectrums of information. Strategy requires focus. It produces a clear set of actions to take and frequently comes with a sense of urgency. Scanning is a process leaders think they can delegate. They don't ever think that way about strategy. The point here is that scanning and planning are very different operations. They must connect, but by careful design.

Some form of environmental scanning takes place prior to or as a part of the strategic planning processes. It some cases it's referred to as a SWOT analysis where the exercise is to identify the association's strengths, weaknesses, opportunities, and threats. The first two components are not really an environmental scan because they focus on internal conditions; but the search for opportunities and threats involves the external environment and might therefore be thought of as a scan. In this context, environmental scanning is not an established program in its own right. It's merely a step in the strategic planning process.

## An Enacted Environment

An environment includes the conditions, circumstances, and influences that surround and affect the viability of a system; be it organism or organization. From the environmental scanner's perspective, there is more going on in an environment than anyone could possibly be aware of, so the term *enacted environment* was coined to capture the notion that the environment you scan is one that you have chosen to be aware of—that is, you enacted it. This is an important concept because it accounts for some important points:

- Many factors in the full environment are prudently eliminated from consideration because they are not relevant and you can't account for everything.

- There are probably relevant factors that you simply don't notice. Realizing it is an enacted environment makes you more aware of the fact that you are looking at a subset of your environment and you may not have all the right parameters.

- And believe it or not, you may be in denial regarding a few very relevant issues that are right in your face, but you've managed to avoid noticing them.

Understanding the enacted environment facilitates two simple but important points. First, you can't be aware of everything in your environment, so by necessity you focus on selected things. Knowing that you've probably filtered out some important elements is like having an open-door policy. It makes it easier for those missing factors to jump into your awareness and surprise you. So set parameters, but remain open minded.

The second point regarding the need to appreciate the implications of an enacted environment has to do with denial, that protective shield we all engage from time to time. It's difficult to know what we don't know, but should know. When associations conduct focus groups with the customers of their members, some of these denial points may be highlighted.

For example, an engineering association invested considerable resources in a public relations campaign to improve public understanding of the fact that engineers are the wonderful folks who provide the technologies that make life so productive and pleasant.

Subsequent focus group research showed that the public already knew this and that they hold engineers in very high regard. However, there was one emerging blemish on the profession's image that hadn't yet registered with them. A growing number of people were beginning to see engineers as technical problem solvers for hire; people who may focus too much on solving problems from the narrow perspective of those who engage their services. The emerging impression—rightly or wrongly held—was that engineers may not be sufficiently attentive to the social implications that stem from their client-centered solutions. Their public relations investment was selling a message the public already knew when it could have addressed an emerging issue that needed a strategy. Unflattering trends are frequently filtered out of the enacted environment due to denial.

## Two Environments to Consider

From the standpoint of scanning, every organization has two environments to consider. You should scan both, but resources may require that you start with one and get to the other eventually. When you do get to both, you need to know if one deserves more attention than the other, which is a formula that may shift over time.

- The **task environment** refers to the immediate conditions that include the organization's market segments and demographics, such as member segments, their customers and beneficiaries, suppliers and competitors, regulators, workforce suppliers, and so forth. You might think of this as a micro environment or a bubble that separates your members and those who have a direct bearing on what they do from the rest of the world.

- The **universal environment** accounts for everything outside your little bubble. There is a lot going on out there, and it is much more difficult to account for than the local task environment that seems so familiar. However, the universe is brewing up all sorts of change out there, and some of it will poke its way through the bubble and rock your world.

To deal with the vast expanse of the universal environment, some categorization tools have been developed. They help organize your thinking by pointing to a few critical few subject areas from which major trends seem to emanate fairly reliably. The two most popular categorizing schemes come with acronyms to help you remember where you should look for trends:

1. STEEP: Social, Technology, Economy, Environment, Politics
2. PESTLE: Politics, Economics, Social, Technological, Legal, Environment

The purpose of these categorical references is to pose questions and identify places to go for answers. For example: *What technological changes are most apt to affect your constituents and how?* This same question is asked for each of the areas. Scanning team members can be assigned specific categories to divide the work and focus people's attention. (See "Monitoring the Environment" in Chapter 3 for more on how this works.)

Scanning the task environment typically produces results that appear to be more relevant, but using that approach alone runs the risk of missing trends that may not currently appear in that environment but are heading your way. Scanning the universal environment addresses that concern, but the information it produces requires additional analysis to understand its relevance.

The prospect of a supply shortage for a critical material used to manufacture goods in the task environment has implications that are immediately apparent. The fact that schools are teaching children differently today and that may deliver a different workforce 10 years from now is something that carries more implications for some occupations that it does for others. Knowing if your industry or profession will be affected and what those effects will be is not readily apparent. Understanding these implications requires additional analysis. (For more on this, see Chapter 3.)

## Environmental Factors

The type of task environment you will scan is influenced by three factors: uncertainty, complexity, and rate of change. Every task environment is unique, but these factors help you analyze that environment in terms that affect the kind of scanning you will need to pursue and the resources it will require.

- **Uncertainty** refers to the level of clarity and predictability associated with the major trends that are being monitored. Information theory puts this concept of uncertainty on a range that runs from unequivocal to equivocal where the former represents information that is certain or highly predictable and the latter represents information that is poorly understood and not predictable. For instance, the health care industry is currently overwhelmed by equivocal information in its environment.

  There are two points each scanner should keep in mind with respect to this. Every task environment has its own uncertainty profile, and it changes over time. A good example is the automobile industry. Automobile manufacturing has a good deal of uncertainty in its environment, but not nearly as much as it did a few decades ago. When globalization of that industry began, the developed countries constituted their own market-places with their own manufacturers. This was inefficient in many respects, one of which was the fact that there was more manufacturing capacity than was required or could survive in a single global market. The shakeout was painful. Uncertainty ruled on issues like which companies would survive, what vehicle types would capture the most market share, how important nationalism would be in purchasing decisions, whether energy costs would ever stabilize, and so on. Most of that has played out now. The move away from petroleum is not yet a reality, but it's begun and now fairly predictable.

  Every scanner's job is to produce information that reduces uncertainty to the greatest extent possible. It is important to know how much information is out there. And yes, everyone says the world is changing so rapidly, and everything seems so uncertain. But no, it's not the same for every industry or profession. Calibrating this is important because the level of uncertainty will influence the resources required to scan the environment and the reasonable levels of expectations people should have for the results.

- **Complexity** accounts for the stratification and diversity of the population you must account for in determining the parameters of the task environment. Every association has its own unique profile. Court reporters are diverse and segmented by legal jurisdictions, specialties, available technologies, and employer types. Still, their segmentation scheme is far less complex than it is for electrical engineers, who work in an enormous range of industries and technologies. Defining a task environment for a profession that includes so many standard industrial classification codes is a complex undertaking.

• **Rate of change,** as the term implies, accounts for the speed with which the environment is generating new issues and morphing the ones already in view. This is closely related to uncertainty because an environment that is changing quickly is probably difficult to predict. The health care industry is loaded with uncertainly, and it is changing rapidly; for now. However, eventually it will stabilize around new healthcare delivery models. Information technologies, on the other hand, are approaching a perfect storm as the already hyperactive pace of IT innovations meets the era of artificial intelligence represented by IBM's Watson program, which beat the experts at "Jeopardy" and is now orchestrating massive amounts of information in fields such as medicine. That industry's rate of change has no end in sight.

## Time Parameters

The final element to consider before launching your scanning process is the time parameters. This includes two factors: whether your process will be ongoing or periodic and how far out in time it will try to reach.

The term *monitoring* suggests an observation process that is constant over time. Gathering is something that's done periodically, like a harvest. Many associations run a fairly ambitious intelligence gathering process just before their periodic planning process, which may happen once every three years. Many people call this environmental scanning, but doing this diminishes an important distinction. Staying ahead of a rapidly changing environment requires an ongoing observation process, which is monitoring.

To constantly monitor an environment that is changing at a moderate pace may constitute a waste of resources. A periodic intelligence gathering process is probably far more appropriate. It's a distinction worth making because monitoring an environment and periodic intelligence gathering operate under very different assumptions and produce substantially different results. So think about your environment, appreciate the distinction, make the right choice, and give it the right name.

How far out in time you intend to look for trends that will affect your industry or profession in the future requires some forethought that is rarely given. Here are some rules of thumb that apply:

- The extent to which you will be able to get out in time is affected by the three environmental attributes complexity, uncertainty, and rate of change. Be realistic.

- Groups typically aspire to get further out in time than they are capable of achieving because uncertainty increases to a level that makes it difficult for people to agree on anything with confidence. Scenario planning is an approach to consider in this situation.

- Groups start by assessing trends everyone can agree on—which means trends affecting them here and now rather than in the future. No matter how far out in time you hope to get, you need to deal with these immediate trends first. Only then can you reach out farther in time. Otherwise, people will keep hounding you about the issues that concern them today.

- If conditions make it difficult to see very far into the future, then it is all the more important to have an ongoing monitoring process that tracks and interprets subtle changes as they occur.

Some of the concepts in this chapter may seem to be a little too theoretical or even esoteric, but scanning the environment is like looking for a needle in a haystack. The task easily becomes overwhelming unless there are some theoretical constructs to help sort things out. These fundamental aspects of scanning are too frequently the things responsible for misunderstandings and differing expectations. If everyone takes the time to clarify their understanding of scanning with respect to these items, they will be ready to roll up their sleeves and design the type of program that meets their collective expectations.

---

## *Before You Start to Scan*

Here is what you need to do before you actually start the scanning process:

1. **Write your own definition of environmental scanning.** Decide what it will do and can accomplish. Then get everyone who expects any outcomes from it to agree.

2. **Decide if you will tackle one or both of the two environments.** If you focus on only one, make sure that is accounted for in your definition and expectation statement. Provide some estimate of when you will be addressing both.

3. **Enact your environment.** For the task environment, that means identifying the players who will be included in your assessment— for example, suppliers, competitors, and so forth. For the universal environment, apply one of the categorization schemes and make an initial estimate of which areas are most apt to produce significant issues.

4. **Finally, estimate your task environment's uncertainty, complexity, and rates of change.** Invite others to challenge your assumptions until there is a reasonable level of agreement.

---

# CHAPTER 3

# Designing and Implementing an Environmental Scanning Process

This chapter addresses the design and implementation of an effective environmental scanning process. There is no one fits-all formula for all associations to follow, so it lays out the fundamentals that all scanning processes ideally should have and provides some details to illustrate how they might work.

## Monitoring the Environment

The terms *monitoring* and *scanning* are sometimes used synonymously, but here they have very different meanings. Scanning is an umbrella term that covers three distinct operations, of which monitoring is one. *Gathering* is sometimes used as a synonym for monitoring, so as you refer to other sources on the subject, be aware of these semantic variations.

The scanning process of any association will over time integrate the three fundamental operations every scanning effort must have in place with some unique approaches that fit the association's particular situation and preferences. The three fundamental operations are:

- **Monitoring** the environment, meaning looking for relevant information that may affect the future viability of the industry/profession and the association.

- **Interpreting** the information to determine why it is relevant, meaning answering the most important question: how will this affect us?

- **Formatting** the information in a manner that makes it **actionable** in the strategic planning process.

## Selecting and Orienting the Monitors

Monitoring an environment in a scanning operation requires more than one person. When only one person is involved, it's really more along the lines of research, much like the work a market analyst does. Some associations have such people on staff, and they are certainly capable of producing excellent information regardless of what their process is called. However, an essential part of scanning is having more than one pair of eyeballs looking for the information and then vetting it to make sure it is considered from different perspectives. This is not only a quality control feature; it is part of the analytics.

When two or more monitors are considering the same information, several questions are implicit. Do they see it the same way, or do they reach different conclusions? If their conclusions are different, why is that? More information may be required to resolve the differences. When a scanning operation makes observations about the future there is always some uncertainly. The vetting process not only serves to refine the information; it can help calibrate the degree of uncertainly.

The number of people who should be involved will vary according to the available resources and the three environmental factors: complexity, uncertainty, and rate of change. For general purposes it is safe to say that three to seven active monitors would constitute a solid scanning operation. Again, for general purposes, assume none of them are fully dedicated to this, but they should have about 10 percent of their time allocated to the scanning activity.

It would be ideal to have the participation of one professional person from each of the information-based program areas, like education, government relations, and publishing. In effect, these people are scanners. They look for changes that warrant new learning objectives, or issues that might need policy decisions, or news worth pursuing. It may be a difficult notion to sell at first, but the fact of the matter is the scanning assignment is an opportunity to improve the work they do in their primary positions; i.e., take advantage of what their fellow scanners are seeing and be the first to capitalize on it in their program areas.

There are many variations on this basic model, which is easier to explore once the different type of players in the scanning process are established. There are generally three: drivers, contributors, and users:

- **Drivers**—the people who design the process and direct the activities

- **Contributors**—the people who actively participate in the scanning process, either by performing scanning functions or simply providing information when scanners ask for it

- **Users**—the people who are involved in strategic planning process and depend on input from the environmental scan to design, deploy, and manage strategies

## Drivers

Drivers of the scanning process are typically from one of three profiles: the CEO, a staff person with assigned responsibility for the function, or a volunteer leader. It's a bit of an overstatement, but association CEOs either have or do not have a natural inclination to scan the environment. When they do, they read more than one paper a day (old school) and/or check various websites regularly. The fact that they see this as a part of their job coincides with the fact that they love to do it. The extent to which they formally analyze and deliver information from their scanning interests may vary greatly, but those who come by it naturally have a compelling need to share the information in some manner.

If a designated staff person is assigned responsibility for driving a scanning process, odds are the individual was chosen for having this natural inclination to be in contact with the world around him or her or the individual has acquired the relevant competencies to do the job as in the case of a librarian or a market researcher.

Volunteer leaders are the least likely people to be real drivers because the work involved typically exceeds any reasonable expectations of volunteers. They may have a driver-like title by virtue of office, like a president-elect who will have the helm in the near future and is therefore thought to be the right person to decipher what the future holds. A pro-forma assignment like this requires a real driver in a support position.

The phrase "naturally inclined" to be a scanner is not used incidentally. Research on environmental scanning recognizes two types that are referred to as social intuitive and formal analytical. Social intuitive simply acknowledges the fact that everyone scans his or her environment for useful information about what's coming down the pike, but some people are much better at it than others. High users of social media are trafficking in the kind of information that lends itself to social-intuitive scanning. The research indicates that founders of successful startup ventures are very adept at social-intuitive scanning. They do a lot of networking and frequently ask questions or stimulate thinking about the future. These are the types of people you want involved in your scanning operation.

The term *formal-analytical* refers to a defined scanning process, which might otherwise be thought of as bringing discipline, range, and reliable output to the social-intuitive impulse. If you drive a scanning process where people investigate a wide range of sources and generate reports on what you find, you're in formal-analytical mode.

Other research into the types of people who perform well in scanning activities suggests attributes to look for:

- **Imagination**—the ability to create mental images of things that have not actually happened. Because the future hasn't happened yet, scanning requires a good deal of this.

- **Fluency**—the ability to speak or write easily and coherently. Scanning is about exploring concepts using language.

- **Networking**—the inclination to develop contacts with a diverse spectrum of people and to stay in touch with them over time. This involves both giving and gathering information.

In addition to these personal attributes, it's good to have at least one representative from each program department who scans as a matter of course, including journalists, lobbyists, and education professionals.

## Contributors

Contributors can be thought of as being either active or passive. Active contributors perform specific functions aimed at finding information in the environment. This might include staff and volunteer committee members who have specific tasks to perform. Retained consultants can be thought of as contributors because they may generate scanning information as a part of their services. However, they usually provide counsel on the types of activities to engage in as a part of the scanning process, which makes them drivers of a certain type. Passive contributors provide information when asked, such as members responding to a survey or participating in a town-hall-type discussion.

There's no standard demographic profile of an association scanning committee or task force, but a productive profile of contributors to the process might include the following:

- **One or two board members.** It's nice to have a liaison who can give some perspective, but it can also make for an uneven discussion if the board is a recipient of the scanning group's report and some but not all are well-versed on the content.

- **CEOs and/or a senior staff people.** Typically they have the best view of the members' world and can keep things in perspective. (They also overcome administrative hurdles marvelously.)

- **Carefully selected, highly involved members who are not officers but probably will be some day.** These people bring two assets: 1) their member perspective on the environment and 2) their ambition with respect to association leadership.

- **"Young" people or other members from segments that are being cultivated for the future.** ASAE's research on the decision to join an association makes it clear that members under 30 see things differently than those who serve at the board level. Since scanning is about the future, it would be good to have some of the people who will be a part of it involved in environmental scanning.

- **Association outsiders from the task environment, such as suppliers or customers of the members.** This is particularly useful when these people work for organizations that do effective scanning or good market research.

## Users

Users are the people who make use of the scanned information. This certainly includes members of a planning committee, and it should involve staff and other committees where people need to be thinking about the future suitability of what they produce or what they should be producing, but aren't yet. Associations that are really good at scanning make this information available to members who value the content for their own scanning purposes. The user profile of the scanning effort should be documented and their needs accounted for in the design of the output (see section on formatting).

## Information to Seek through Scanning

So what are you looking for when you scan an environment? There are various taxonomies, syntaxes, or organizing methods for this, and they go by many different names. One such method is reviewed here because it seems relevant to the information associations seek.

It distinguishes events, trends, and issues. An event is a happening or occurrence of something that seems important or at least noteworthy. It could be a unique meeting that was held that raised a topic or drew an audience that was unique in some way. Events are rarely more than noteworthy, but that means they are deserving of a note being made somewhere. For example, someone sponsors an event where students in a particular profession are invited to work very hard in a developing nation for an entire summer at close to no salary whatsoever, and the sponsors are astonished to find that they get far more volunteers than expected. This should be a noteworthy event to the professional society that pertains to this population, and it is noteworthy because they had nothing to do with it and offer nothing along those lines.

The most interesting events in a scanning operation are those that turn out to be harbingers of the future. Knowing if a single event is a harbinger is a speculative business at best, but once a string of similar events occur over time, there may be legitimate reason to think the environment is percolating some kind of significant change. When an event is noted, that means the scanners are on alert to see if a similar type of event happens again.

A trend is a string of events that builds momentum over time as it develops increasingly significant implications for anyone in its path. For example, back in the 80s, before the establishment of the World Wide Web, people began to notice that technology geeks were connecting desktop computers to phone lines and posting information on bulletin boards for others to read and respond to at their pleasure. For most of us, it began with a single instance about which we heard. Then there were a string of them. Then there was an internet. Then the U.S. Postal Service was in jeopardy because people don't write letters like they used to. Who saw it coming? How soon did they see it? How well did they adapt?

An issue is the outcome of the interpretation process that recognizes a trend and answers that previously cited critical question: How will that affect us? In our postal example, if you were part of the association representing the small-press printing industry that produced all those newsletters every other association sent to their members on a monthly basis, the issue was straightforward: *The internet's rapidly expanding ability to convey news instantaneously and at no cost beyond the gathering and writing expenses will reduce demand for printing services to a degree that will put most of our members out of business.* That's what converting a trend into an issue looks like. (See the formatting material for more information on constructing a strategic issue.)

The purpose of a scanning operation is to look for meaningful events, track them, and recognize if and when they become significant trends, and then decipher the specific implications for the association and its members.

## Identifying Sources of Information for Scanning

Determining which information sources an association scanning operation should look to is probably the most unique and highly customized part of the business. Here are some rules of thumb to help find your way to the right ones:

1. **Develop three categories of sources.** Include those sources you scan on a regular basis, sources you check in on occasionally,

and some serendipitous means of bouncing around the universe hoping to bump into something.

2. **Don't limit your routine to established sources like print media and internet sources.** For example, meetings that your members go to are excellent sources. The staff members at one association get together prior to their annual meeting and agree on three to five questions they will ask members whenever they get a chance, such as at luncheons and receptions. When they return from the meeting, they get together for about an hour and share what they learned from this inquiry. That's a form of scanning. See if you can get some scanners to attend meetings that your members' customers, clients, or patients attend. In a similar manner, tap into their suppliers.

3. **Differentiate your regular sources from your occasional ones.** Big name, no brainers: Sources you check on a regular basis will certainly include a thoughtful list of highly credible news sources such as *The New York Times,* online and/or print. If your membership is not all that impacted by finances and the economy, you still need to have some of these sources on your regular list, but if *The Wall Street Journal* is your regular, then other financially oriented sources can go on your occasional list.

4. **Survey your members to identify the top five information sources they go to and make sure you are tracking them as well.** In the survey, make sure you differentiate between general news and industry or profession sources.

## Establish a Monitoring Routine

The ongoing work for the core scanning team of about four to seven people will be some variation on the following exercise and schedule:

- Each member of the team takes lead responsibility for following sources from the official scanning list. Other than that, they are encouraged to wander anywhere they like.

- A regular meeting schedule (i.e. monthly) is established for the team to meet. The length of the meeting should be set and disciplined, perhaps 60 to 90 minutes.

- In a round-robin fashion, each member of the team is expected to put some new observations on the table for discussion. At the end of the meeting, the team leader reads a short list of items he or she believes should be added to the monitoring record, which that person keeps. Team members are encouraged to challenge those assumptions. The rule of thumb: Add anything anyone is adamant about.

- The structure of the record follows whatever taxonomy is adopted, such as the previously mentioned one that includes events, trends, and issues.

- At some regular interval, the record that builds from these sessions is vetted further in the interpretation process.

## Interpreting the Environment

The purpose of the monitoring process is to accurately identify trends that may have significant impact on the future of the industry/profession and the association. The purpose of the interpretation process is to accurately decipher what those impacts will be and craft them as issue statements. *"The tumbling granite might hit you,"* says the monitor. *"But is it a stone that could cut my leg or a boulder that will crush my skull?"* asks the interpreter. Monitoring picks up on forces that drive change. Interpreting predicts consequences.

## The Interpretation Process

The scanning team monitors the enacted environment, identifies events and trends thought to be worth tracking, and has preliminary discussions on the issues that the association should address in the strategic planning process, but more than one group should be asked to consider why and how an issue may affect the organization's viability in the future.

This is a sequential process that starts with the scanners and goes on to include encounters with other groups, each of which is asked to challenge the thinking of those who preceded them. The exercise for each encounter is essentially the same, though the specific steps may vary to accommodate the venue and group demographics. The participants are presented with five to eight statements for discussion that characterize the trends that are developing in a way that is apt to alter the way work is done or value is delivered by the industry or profession. The statements do not specify any consequences that the change may have on the affected parties, which in this case is the association's membership.

---

### An Example of Statements as Change Agents

An oncology association might pose the following statement as a change agent:

*Pharmaceutical science is moving cancer treatments from clinical infusions that only oncologists can provide to oral medicines that any physician can prescribe.*

The participants in discussions about the statement would be asked three questions that are the same for all change agents:

- Do you think that this is an accurate statement?
- How significant a change is this in terms of level of impact on the industry/profession?
- What consequences will this change bring to bear on your business/ work/career?

If the first two questions don't produce strong responses, the third is moot, so go on the next change agent statement. Although there are three questions, note that there are only two variables, and with each encounter, you are trying to refine your understanding of them:

1. A force that is driving significant change.
2. Consequences this change may have for a particular group of people.

---

Here is one configuration on how this process of sequential discussions led by the scanning team might work.

- **Meet in person or by conference call at some regular interval— say monthly or quarterly—to discuss what each member has observed since the last meeting.** Since this might involve a considerable amount of information, people should provide a written summary in advance so that others can express opinions on what warrants a group discussion. Exercises should be in place to brainstorm the possible implications of a given issue.

- **Find a trial balloon audience to whom to present these work-in-progress findings.** A staff meeting is an excellent venue for this. Don't overwhelm them. Address three to five issues by presenting the scanning team's thinking on why each of the issues is important and how it may affect the members and the association. Repeat this drill as necessary.

  Don't restrict this exercise to an established meeting of department heads. If it is a large association, expand it to include all program managers who have any kind of window on the world of the members. Think of the exercise as being more than feedback on scanning. The term *organizational learning* refers to what everyone knows and the knowledge they are in positions to acquire. This exercise feeds that inquisition and legitimizes the importance of their perspective and the value of what they can contribute. It stimulates organizational learning.

- **Present the possible change agents to a group of members.** Once your preliminary analysis is refined as a result of a trial balloon group, it is ready for prime time. If you are creative, the possible venues for this are extensive. They might include:

  - A town hall gathering or a series of focus groups at the annual meeting. As the single largest gathering of members in one place and at one time, the annual meeting is an inexpensive way to conduct focus groups with the members, which also makes it the most productive way to vet the scan.

  - Twenty-minute feedback sessions with every committee that meets in the course of the year. This might be a productive use of their lunch time. They need a break from what they have been talking about, and scanning information can provoke a lively conversation that they appreciate.

  - An online conversation about the future. New online services now available are made to either revolutionize associations as a conversational forum or replace them. Hundreds, even thousands, of people can comment on issues in a way that self-organizes a discussion in a manner that provides massive member input to the interpretive process of scanners and does so in a way that participants find to be an intellectually rewarding experience. This technology is easily and inexpensively available to associations of all sizes.

In this manner, the interpretation process is refining a series of cause-and-effect statements that may warrant strategic attention. While the ultimate goal is to identify and accurately characterize strategic issues that a planning committee should address, there is one caveat worth noting in this quest for the really big issues. Watch out for issues that drop to the bottom because they are not thought to be very probable; conceivable maybe, but not very probable.

Most of these should drop to the bottom, but before you let that happen, ask one additional question. If it did happen, would it be a game-changer? If this question gets an affirmation, don't take too much time discussing it, but don't let it drop. Remember it. Address it briefly in subsequent discussions to see if there is consensus on its game-changer status. If it is a wild card, keep bringing it out for the primary purpose of parking it in people's heads. Park in enough of these places, and it becomes a collective sub-conscious radar screen. Any future indications that it might be happening may provoke a response that you actually hear.

## The Politics of Interpretation and Leadership Commitment

Planning committees are the ultimate recipients of this information, and they're made up of important people who have the stature to dismiss anything in a scanning report that their immediate reaction doesn't find to be a legitimate concern. ASAE's research and publication *The Decision to Join* shows unequivocally that these same leaders are not always in sync with member thinking—for reasons that are both good and questionable. The primary purpose of rank-and-file member input in the interpretation process is to vet the analysis with input from people who will be affected by the change agents in question. A secondary but important purpose is to give the prognosis the stature it needs to withstand immediate dismissal.

An association that initiates a scanning process may only be giving lip service to the latest fad—at first. Over time the scanning function either fades away or is institutionalized into standard operations. The difference lies in the value it delivers. One study of scanning in the private sector showed that senior management thought much of the information produced was outdated, too narrow in scope, and not very useful. For leaders to be committed, they must understand that it may take three or more annual cycles to develop a highly valued scanning process.

## Assessing the Quality of Scanning Outputs

The value and long-term success of an environmental scanning process should be determined at two different points. The first is when the report is put into the hands of the association's strategic planning committee. The second comes years later when everybody involved has enough hindsight to determine the accuracy and significance of the predictions. Obviously there's a catch to this. If the initial scanning reports are not good enough to pass the first test, the scanning effort won't be around long enough to face the second. So let's deal with first things first.

Quality is said to reside in a product or service's fitness-for-use. Quality is thought to be present if a product or service does what it is supposed to do in a manner that is efficient and effective. The quality of an environmental scanning report is determined by the fitness-for-use it has as an input to the strategic planning process. This is an engineering concept, and there's only one problem with it. If the strategic planning process is poorly defined, and many of them are, then generating a useful scanning report can be a difficult target to hit.

To address this, scan drivers should certainly ask the strategy makers what they need in terms of a reporting format. If the planning process is poorly defined in terms of the tasks that will be performed and the materials that will be required, then they'll probably respond with a ramble on what they *like* in a report. If it is a well-defined process, they'll specify what they *need*. At this point, you're looking at three possible scenarios:

- They specify what they need, and you give it to them.

- They ramble on, so you give them what you think is a good format, but brace yourself for criticism when their process doesn't go so well.

- You give them an outline of a strategy-making process that includes clear specifications on how scanning outputs should be formatted to fit neatly into the fabrication of a strategy.

Chapter 5 describes a strategy management process—as opposed to a strategic planning process—that takes a more contemporary view of an ongoing strategy-making process that is fueled by environmental scanning and specifies the way outputs from scanning should be formatted to accommodate inputs for strategy.

---

### *Four Key Points to Establishing and Managing a Scanning Process*

1. In forming a core team of scanners, draw people from the program areas that already scan (by some other name) and see to it that the scanning assignment enhances their "real job" performance.

2. Establish a system or syntax to sort and record scanned information in a manner that is consistent and useful.

3. Vet the scanned information with multiple groups of people to refine it, to enlighten them, and to give the final report credibility.

4. Understand how the planning process works and make sure the scanning report fits those needs.

---

# CHAPTER 4
# Getting Started

In the preceding chapters, we've outlined the rationale for scanning, presented the case that it is essential for associations, especially those that operate in a rapidly changing environment, to establish a well-defined scanning process, and introduced best practices for establishing a scanning process. Your scanning team should include a wide range of individuals, including staff, volunteer members, and a few board members, and they should look at a wide range of information sources from print and digital media to member surveys and transcripts of member town-hall meetings. They should also look outside the organization to customers, vendors, and competitors.

Equally important is an interpretation stage where issues identified during the scan are discussed for possible implications and ramifications. It is at this stage where the membership can prove to be very helpful. Just having staff sort through the issues leaves the association vulnerable to group think and also makes it easier for the board or the strategic planning committee to dismiss the results of the scan. However, if the membership is included in the scanning process through attendance at town hall meetings or participation in mini-surveys, for example, then there is a higher likelihood that there will be feedback from members to the board on some issues, helping to focus the association's leadership on those issues that may become trends.

In the next chapter, we will examine the crucial role the board or strategic planning committee plays in crafting a response to the trends that emerge from the environmental scanning process. But first, let's look at the experiences of some associations in their scanning processes.

## Examples of Environmental Scanning

The Credit Union National Association (CUNA) is known for its extensive environmental scanning to spot potential trends. The organization's environmental scanning is assembled annually into several products to help member credit unions and those credit unions' boards of directors make sense of the current environment and trends on the horizon. These products are also a source of revenue for the association.

They include the *E-Scan Report,* a printed book of more than 100 pages, a DVD in the format of a news program which highlights the material in the *E-Scan Report,* and PowerPoint slides of the material in the book. These are offered for sale to credit unions and the public at retail prices ranging from $95 for the book to $240 for the DVD or the PowerPoint slides. CUNA also offers other tools to help credit unions stay current with trends and facilitate their strategic planning efforts, including a subscription to an e-scan newsletter (Free to book purchasers, this e-newsletter updates the book when new issues emerge.) and a *Strategic Planning Guide.* There is also information from the book on CUNA's website and information from the updates is posted there, too.

The *E-Scan Report* is researched and written by experts working in their particular areas, such as legislative and regulatory issues, marketing, business trends, economics, and human resources for about a dozen chapters in all. CUNA's advocacy office in Washington, D.C., writes the legislative and regulatory chapter with the help of their state offices to provide the state-level perspective, and CUNA's senior economists write the chapter on economic outlook.

CUNA has a research department that fields surveys ranging from comprehensive assessments designed to measure satisfaction with programs and services to mini-surveys asking for a quick take of what threats members perceive. Taking the member's pulse on topics helps to guide article selection and direction in CUNA publications and placement of issues by their advocacy office. CUNA hosts many email lists, blogs, and virtual communities; staff members are very involved in the give and take on issues there, and from this exchange they become aware of new potential issues. They host town-hall meetings at their annual meetings and have avenues ranging from a simple phone call to participation on committees for members to contribute their opinions.

CUNA's national board of directors goes through a strategic planning process annually to review the association's three-year strategic plan. CUNA brings in a facilitator to help the board through the strategic planning process. The board goes through a SWOT analysis and engages in a discussion of whether any new potential trends are valid and likely to have an impact on the credit union environment, what the implications of the new trends might be, and what CUNA's response should be to the likely new trend. The strategic planning session is held in June every year. The new plan goes into effect in January and is again reviewed in June. This is continuous environmental scanning at a grand scale.

Your association might more closely resemble the National Ground Water Association. NGWA has members who work for very large multinational corporations and members who own small businesses whose work seldom takes them 50 miles from their home location. NGWA staff is challenged by the reality that these very different sectors of the membership have trouble understanding the concerns of the other group. NGWA has both populations represented on its board, and it can be challenging to get the international represen-tatives to empathize with the local concerns of the small business owners and vice versa. Staff members persevere by presenting the issues and challenges in different ways using different terminology to meet this challenge.

The small business owner members are struggling to stay alive in a very tough economic environment. They don't feel like they have the time to engage in a discussion on trends that may influence the future. NGWA's exec has this same challenge at times with his board. He prepares a monthly digest of all that's out there for his board, the issue and its strategic implications to get them thinking about it. He expects them to read the digest, think about it, and discuss it with members in the field. Sometimes, however, the trends discussion doesn't gain traction.

The experiences of these two associations illustrate the range of environments that association executives can face. Still, both of these examples highlight established practices, which begs the question, how does an association executive who is new to environmental scanning get started?

## How to Get Started

As we've outlined earlier, your scanning process should be well-defined. Careful thought should go into the composition of the scanning team to ensure that multiple talents are on hand. The simple fact is that some people are better suited to the abstract nature of information collection than others, and some have more patience and better skills at sifting through the glut of information that is available. Careful thought should also go into identifying sources of information.

Don't neglect your membership in your scanning activities. Not only may you find willing volunteers to help you sort through all the information that is out there, you will need the membership to sort through the issues that are identified from your scanning activities. Early involvement will almost certainly lead to better results. Some association execs we spoke to in telephone interviews have found that member volunteers have taken on vital roles in the scanning process, such as monitoring social media websites, responding where appropriate, and reporting back to staff what is being discussed and what issues are emerging.

A very good source for potential trends is the town-hall meeting; open sessions at the end of regularly scheduled membership meetings often result in grist for the scanning mill.

It also may be productive to take a look at what other associations have identified as trends. Here some other steps that you can take to facilitate environmental scanning at your association.

### Identify critical trends and assess their impact.

Start by reviewing the "50 Key Trends" on the ASAE website at www.asaecenter.org/spi/sia.cfm and other materials there. Not all of these materials will have relevance to your organization, but a review of them will get you thinking strategically. Also, check out the Scan to Plan Interactive tool; the description of how this process works could also get you thinking strategically, and consider signing up and going through the formal SPI process with your board or strategic planning committee. A sober analysis of whether any one of the 50 key trends will have an impact on your organization is a very good start to the scanning process.

Internet searches are sure to reveal what other associations have identified as trends affecting their enacted environment. It is good practice to think of all these trends in the context of your association. Bat these trends around among your staff to get them thinking about the environmental scanning process.

### *Ask the member.*

How can you identify additional trends that may affect your association? If you haven't set up and publicized procedures to enable members to communicate their concerns, make this a top priority. Your members are your eyes and ears in their local communities, and you want to foster an environment of easy two-way communication between members, staff, and volunteer leaders. Your organizational culture may dictate the best method to accomplish this. For instance, virtual communities may not be the best fit for a membership that is computer-challenged.

Establish multiple channels for receiving feedback through phone calls, dedicated (and constantly monitored) email addresses where members submit information on trends, email lists, webpages, town-hall sessions at regularly scheduled meetings, focus groups, or surveys. The important element to remember is that this should be a conversation, a back-and-forth dialogue among staff, leadership, and members about the future. It helps to identify issues and establish a forward-thinking environment. It is an excellent way to draw in new members, who will probably be excited by a discussion about the future of the trade or profession they've entered. Establish processes for staff to enter into a searchable database the feedback they get from calls or messages and set up regular staff meetings where member complaints and concerns are discussed. Do your part to foster a climate where ideas, no matter how off-the-wall they seem, get a fair and complete hearing.

Many associations hold town-hall sessions at their meetings to give members another means of providing feedback. Many executives are very keen on town-hall meetings. They say that the information shared during them is often more valuable than the scheduled agenda of the meeting. Even when town-hall sessions haven't been on the agenda, these executives speak of hanging around after meetings and engaging members one-on-one to find out what is on their minds.

Get your publications involved by having them feature articles about the new procedures you've established to capture members' concerns, the new forward-focused theme the association is establishing, or a preview of a series of focus groups you're planning to discuss the future of the profession. Generate activity on your website by making the links to pages where members can speculate about the future a prominent feature on your home page. Keep updating the site and the articles to show that this is an ongoing process and that it is important to have member input in the direction it takes. Make your members feel valued for their contributions and extend that sentiment to staff and volunteers as well.

Are there external constituencies that are important to your association? Reach out to them in a similar fashion. Vendors, suppliers, trade press, and even competitors could be good sources of information and may be well-positioned to spot trends that could affect your association. Possible ways to gather feedback from outside constituencies could include phone calls, email lists, surveys, focus groups, or virtual communities.

### Target your information sources carefully.
Feedback from members adds significantly to the first step of an environmental scan: collecting information or monitoring. Formalize this process by establishing processes for systematically paying attention to the information that flows in. Obviously, you should be paying closest attention to trade publications and information sources related to your field or specialty, but it's also a good idea to monitor national, technology, and business mass media sources such as *The Wall Street Journal, Harvard Business Review, Wired,* or *Popular Science.* You can't keep up with everything. Divvy up pieces of the information flow to staff or volunteers, but make certain that the process includes digests or other reports about what is appearing

in all of the sources out there. Ask staff members and volunteers what information sources they're paying attention to and incorporate those into the process.

Discuss with colleagues and friends what information sources they're paying attention to. Bounce ideas around with peers, using ASAE as a resource for contacts. Since this information is already flowing in, why not establish an ongoing process to formalize the activities and make monitoring and forward thinking parts of the staff mission and incorporate specific functions related to monitoring into position descriptions? Anyone with an internet connection knows that the supply of information is limitless. No one can keep up with even a fraction of it. Fortunately, there are many tools to filter out the irrelevant and ridiculous. Many companies offer aggregating services for a fee, and there are also sites that offer these digests for free. Many websites allow users to create protocols that gather and filter information for free. Search sites make it easy to conduct your own key-word searches, and these can be automated to occur on daily, weekly, or other periodic timetables. RSS feeds are another way to monitor the reams of information that may be relevant to your mission.

### Don't forget social media.
A growing source of information (and misinformation) is social media. Many of the association executives interviewed revealed that their associations became aware of social media through younger staff members, who convinced the top echelon that this was a phenomenon that could not be ignored. If you are not aware of what is being said on social media about your products, industry, or field of interest, you are missing an opportunity to respond to criticism and opening up a hornet's nest of misinformation. It is time-consuming, yes, but it is worth the investment of time and resources to protect your turf on the wild world of the internet. It is also an excellent way to engage younger staff members in important work and reinforce the forward-thinking theme. Some association execs with small staffs have found that volunteers can capably carry out this function, being ever mindful of the imperative that staff be kept informed of issues that arise so that they can track them.

### Become a data-driven organization.

Whether they are quick mini-surveys asking "what is keeping you up at night?" or more comprehensive evaluations of products and services, the data collected from surveying members and others can provide a solid foundation upon which boards can make informed decisions, and staff can receive verification of their hunches, which can empower them to push ahead. To cite one example, the Georgia Society of Association Executives heard from members that there was a lack of good professional development programs in the Atlanta area and Georgia. GSAE fielded a comprehensive survey to determine to what degree this perception was shared among the membership and area association professionals in general.

The association's research showed that there was indeed broad agreement on this lack of programs. Staff and the board realized that this was a void that the GSAE was qualified to fill. The board had the data to show that their adoption of a strategy to provide professional development programs would probably meet with success. With all in agreement, a new professional development project was launched and has proven to be popular, economically successful, and reinforcing to GSAE's brand identity of providing quality services for association professionals. It has helped in recruiting new members, too.

Many association executives who participated in telephone interviews for this book offered this advice to associations just starting out in environmental scanning: Conduct a member survey to find out what is important to the members. Not only does it provide a picture of what the members want, it also establishes a baseline against which progress can be measured. Good data are invaluable to informing your efforts.

### Encourage a culture of foresight.

As stated earlier, unless your field of professional interest or area of specialty can anticipate a slow rate of change, it makes sense to establish a formal, ongoing monitoring process. A good process can help to tame the information stream, clarify staff and leadership roles, and make everybody aware of the importance of thinking into the future of the association.

To further solidify the importance of forward-thinking in your association, establish a "future wall" where staff can post ideas they've read about or concerns they've heard from members; devote time in staff meetings to discuss ideas posted on the future wall, making sure to add ideas that gain some traction to your interpretation process.

Take advantage of the available tools to help you keep track of information flowing in. There are stand-alone products that can help staff enter complaints, comments, and conversations from members; format these open-ended discussions to allow for content analysis searches of topics; and enable staff to generate reports that document words that are turning up frequently in conversations. You need a means to capture notes of staff's conversations with members.

## Then What?

What happens to this information that comes in? What processes are in place to deal with this information? In many associations senior staff collect information relevant to their areas of focus (say communications or advocacy by those respective departments), and as a group they, along with other staff members, evaluate this information for relevance. The information that rises to a level of concern among the staff needs to be further interpreted by another entity that includes rank-and-file members, especially if the association also establishes an ongoing planning process.

Committees are very useful in this task. Think of a discussion session of issues that may have an impact on future operations as a value-added proposition to regular committee activities; it can engage younger members in ways that mundane committee business may not and perhaps groom them for more challenging roles in the association. If meetings are a regular part of association business, hosting an open forum to discuss potential issues can be very valuable, both in weeding out some issues and presenting new ones that the staff overlooked or dismissed. Establish email lists or collaborative communities where ideas are posted and members are asked to assess the potential of those issues in terms of how they might impact the future of the association.

Another means of gathering member input is through the mini-survey; you could ask a sample of members to rate a list of four or six potentially emerging issues for relevance and potential impact. A pre-assessment by some segment of the membership prior to the formal assessment by the strategic planning committee provides another check on relevance and another important step in the process. It is correct and useful for a committee or ad-hoc group of members to parse the information prior to the board focusing on it, especially when a board member is on the committee or participates in the discussion.

What is the format for interpreting the issues? As discussed in the previous chapter, the discussions held at the interpreting stage should focus solely on a cause-and-effect dialectic: whether the issue presents a challenge or opportunity to the association in the future and what the consequences will be if the issue does affect the future. The participants at the interpreting stage do not have the authority to discuss strategies to mitigate impacts or capitalize on opportunities. It will be challenging enough to reach consensus of the cause-and-effect statements of issues. Trying to reach too far at this stage will only complicate matters and muddy the outcome.

## Where the Board Plays a Role

Once consensus has been reached regarding a list of potential issues of concern, it is the responsibility of the strategic planning committee or the board of directors to assess those issues and determine the proper course of action to either mitigate the impact of an issue or take advantage of a new development or technology. The board or committee may reject the issue as unlikely to happen or unlikely to have an impact on the association, but it is essential that they have the discussion about the list of potential trends they've been sent. Refer again to the previous chapter for more discussion on this process.

Often in smaller associations, it is the executive director who is responsible for collecting the information, assembling the board packet, and presenting it to the board. Several of the telephone interviewees expressed concern about their difficulty in getting the board to think strategically about the issues and concerns. In some instances much work went into the preparation of potential trends, which were sent to board members so that they could digest the information prior to the board meeting. At the meeting, however, it became clear that the board members had not done their homework. The executives were not able to get the board to assess the implications of the potential threats, and instead spent much of the meeting discussing operational matters.

Developing a strong culture of thinking about the future may be difficult in tough economic times. In addition to being board members of associations, these individuals have other responsibilities. By the very nature of the association, its board may be business owners who are struggling to keep their companies viable and pay salaries. What is keeping them up at night is, where is my next contract coming from and how will I keep paying my employees? Looking over the horizon for imagined threats is going to take a back seat to the 800-pound gorilla in the room.

Still, it is the responsibility of every association executive to respond to members' concerns and to be on the lookout for potential threats or opportunities. The executive may find himself or herself pushing against barriers internally, but push he or she must, keeping in mind that it is usually not a good idea to get too far in front of the board. Careful environmental scanning can provide answers to seemingly intractable problems and can identify potential avenues of revenue for members.

Hopefully, the end result of this continual pushing is a change in culture. Over time board members move away from an "I already know everything; we don't need to do this" attitude into a "push up the sleeves, let's get started" approach to environmental scanning and strategic planning.

Another positive outcome of environmental scanning can be increased relevance. One executive said that his association changed its focus from telling members how good they were to actually doing things of value to members as identified through their scanning activities. A key component to that was flexibility. Through comprehensive surveys, the organization identified what was affecting its members and worked to bring about new approaches to address the issues.

So, how does an association executive get a recalcitrant board to take up the discussion of trends? One suggestion from *Designing Your Future* is to have board members engage in an exercise called "Mapping Your Personal Future." This exercise is contained as an appendix later in this book. The purpose is to get a board member to project personal goals and ambitions into the future to instill a future focus prior to thinking about the future of the association.

Include at least one board member in the discussion of potential issues during the interpretation stage. The danger here is that this individual may have too much invested in the potential trends and dominate the conversation too much, but it is also possible that this board member will prod and poke his colleagues to do their homework prior to the meeting, call members and encourage them to call other board members with concerns, and further stimulate discussion prior to the meeting.

More board members involved in the interpretation process is probably a good thing. If you are successful in establishing an environment where members are freely communicating with board members, then certainly concerns about the future are being shared. Establish avenues where informal issues' discussions can be tracked, such as on listservers or virtual communities, and have board members involved in these discussions. One piece of advice was that it is much better to help shape emerging issues through early engagement than to wait too long and have to react. The more time the board or strategic planning committee devotes to discussing the implications of emerging trends and what policies can be put in place to address those implications, the better.

A forward-thinking focus can also be a recruiting tool. Young professionals who learn of discussions about the future of the profession by the association will naturally be drawn out of self-interest; if they find that it is easy to participate through committee activities or virtual discussion groups, membership dues may soon be forthcoming.

Another approach could be to include another step in the process: Take the results of the strategic planning process back to the membership. Have board members explain their reasoning behind their decisions and ask members whether they agree with the results. Having to face the membership will certainly add importance to the strategic planning process.

CHAPTER 5

# Strategy Management

*Note: This chapter is an update of material that first appeared in one of ASAE's earlier publications on trends, From Scan to Plan. It describes an ongoing "strategy management" process that many associations are moving to in lieu of the traditional approach to strategic planning. It relates to the formatting suggestions made in Chapter 3. By design, this strategy-making process uses strategic issues, formatted as cause-and-effect statements, as one of four basic parts in the development of strategy.*

Environmental scanning has two potential customers: 1) members who need insight on the future for their own individual planning purposes and 2) staff and volunteers responsible for leading the association's efforts to adjust its products and services based on the collective needs of the entire membership. Serving the first customer is a matter of offering one report that is generic enough to address countless variations in the way members go about planning in their own enterprise. For the second customer, the association, there should be nothing generic about it. As mentioned earlier in the book, the scanning report that goes to the association's planning process should have "fitness for use," which means the output from the scanning process should be customized to meet the requirements of the planning process.

Unfortunately, strategic planning, which by the mid-1990s had evolved into one fairly standard process that nearly every organization followed, has morphed into countless variations as well. So the challenge for environmental scanners is to first determine how strategic planning works in their organizations and then make sure the scanning outputs fit that process. To make that investigation into the planning process, it might help to examine how and why planning has changed as much as it has.

## Changing Nature of Strategic Planning

The notion that strategic planning isn't what it used to be is now widely accepted. Unfortunately, there's much less agreement on what it has become. A symposium held at MIT's Sloan School of Management looked back at strategic planning's 40-year evolution from a cutting-edge concept in the early 1960s through its calcification into a fixed template that inadequately addressed the need for flexibility in rapidly changing environments. In the leading MBA programs, the subject has evolved to a point where the term *strategic planning* rarely appears in either the titles of the courses or the textbooks students use.

The association executive's awareness of this changing perspective on planning was documented in a series of focus groups done as a part of an ASAE Foundation research project that led to the publication of *From Scan to Plan: Managing Change in Associations* (2004). When asked to describe their thoughts on the subject, focus group participants made the following observations:

- There was a point in the not-too-distant past when everyone used a similar approach to planning, but there is no longer any uniform understanding of how it should work.

- Making strategy, by whatever name or process one prefers, must be far more inclusive than before, yet faster and more flexible.

- Some means of anticipating the future and building consensus on what should be done about it is essential.

These three observations pretty well summarize the current challenge. There is no longer any single template for all, but every association must engage a broader spectrum of people in a dialogue on how the environment is changing and how the association and its profession or industry should adapt. And in this adaptive framework one point is clear: Having a strategy is more important than having a document called "The Plan." The concept of strategy and the process of strategy-making are front and center.

## Good Strategy Evolves Gradually

The need to reconsider our understanding of making strategy in rapidly changing conditions is captured by James Brian Quinn, a management guru from Dartmouth's Tuck School of Business, in what he calls logical incrementalism. Quinn says that the development of strategy in successful organizations is not at all like the rational-analytical systems portrayed in the management literature. He thinks it is fragmented, evolutionary, and intuitive. Good strategy evolves over time in a stream of activities that include conversations, planning, serendipity, failed initiatives, persistence, more conversation, and, yes, technique.

This last element may seem to be at odds with the mix that preceded it. If technique is understood to be a systematic procedure by which a complex task is accomplished, isn't it a bit like that rational-analytical system that Quinn and others seem to reject? Yes and no. In the traditional approach to strategic planning, a large batch of information is poured into a rational-analytical model, and a plan is produced. In this alternative, which might be thought of as strategy management, a rational-analytical technique is applied to a flow of information that percolates through a wide variety of events and yields strategies.

An illustration of this can be found in Chapter 3's description of the way scanned information is filtered and refined through a series of venues like staff meetings, focus groups, and town hall sessions at annual meetings. In the initial stages of these events, only one question is raised: Is this an environmental change we should be addressing? This refines your understanding of the issue and confirms its importance. Gradually, the conversation shifts to the second question: What should we do about it?

Two models illustrate how this process might work in an association context. The first provides an overall framework that distinguishes strategic initiatives from established programs. The second puts the concept of strategy into a consistent format that captures its dynamism and makes it easily manageable.

*Figure 1*

Figure 1 illustrates the framework used to distinguish strategic initiatives from ongoing programs. This is important because too often that which is said to be strategic includes an assortment of items that include new initiatives, established activities, programs that need strengthening, and even some very tactical to-dos. This inconsistency is made worse by what is missing. Most of the ongoing programs that deliver value to the customer are not accounted for or are referred to dismissively as being a part of ongoing operations. Even if there is an operating plan that makes them explicit, rarely is there a systematic connection between established programs in an operating plan and new strategic initiatives. The bearing one has on the other is not incidental.

In this framework there are two dimensions: vertical and horizontal. The vertical dimension represents the stable portion of an association. In this dimension, the mission and goals give purpose and direction to the programs that deliver value to customers in the current budget year. These programs have what might be thought of as rolling momentum: cyclical activities that generate value year after year.

Although the content delivered by programs, such as the annual meeting or the magazine change with each edition, their function and purpose are consistent over time. The managers of these programs will adjust them on a regular basis in what is thought of as continuous improvement, but the basic value proposition is stable. Even programs with high variability, like government relations, are fairly stable in terms of their purpose, execution, and resource requirements. As a rule of thumb, 80 to 90 percent of an organization's resources go into these stable, established activities.

The horizontal dimension portrays a dynamic that is the opposite of stability. In this dimension we identify the strategic issues that drive the need for significant change and the initiatives that are launched to address them. The improvements that program managers make in the vertical dimension deal with the effectiveness of their programs. The strategic initiatives in the horizontal dimension change the fundamental nature of the value that the association delivers. To adapt in this significant a manner means managers must surrender their coveted process stability and enter into periods of uncertainty while things get redesigned. New programs may be created, established ones may morph into something else, and in some cases these adaptations may alter the mission and goals of the organization.

Management and leadership in this framework are opposite but complementary functions. We manage to accomplish specific objectives on time and on budget. We lead to help people see the need for change, arrive at a shared vision, and deal with uncertainty as we explore the best way of achieving it. These efforts account for the other 10 to 20 percent of the organization's total resources.

Peter Drucker came to believe that organizations should have two budgets: 1) an operating budget that allocates resources to established programs during a set period and 2) a strategic budget that allocates resources for adaptations that address the future viability of the organization and play out over an unpredictable period. This is not a contingency fund for issues that may come up. It is for strategic initiatives that must come up and are constantly under consideration.

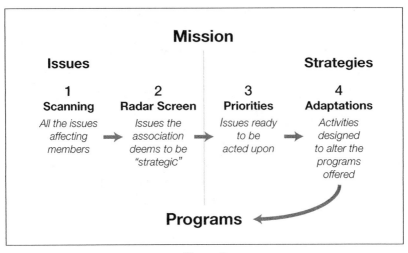

*Figure 2*

The horizontal dimension symbolizes the crosscurrents of change, and it lays out a spectrum of events, as seen in Figure 2, that move from initial efforts to see the forces of change to understanding them and setting priorities and then acting on them. Environmental scanning is used to identify these change agents. The methods of conducting a scan include formal future studies, market research, brainstorming sessions with leaders, town hall conversations with rank-and-file members, and focus groups with member suppliers, clients, and/or customers.

The challenge in managing these activities lies in the highly varied types of information that they must consider. Studies produce recommendations. Some methods of analysis produce lists. Market trends render data. Conversations generate observations. All of this information needs to flow across the horizontal dimension in a sorting and refining process that clarifies, compares, and selects critical information that deserves strategic attention. In the end, a few highly refined issues will compete for limited strategy-making resources.

## Strategic Issues Emerge from Information Overload

Critical to this process is the concept of a strategic issue, which is the interaction of two variables that are affecting each other in ways that demand your attention. A strategic issue is expressed in a

# From Scanning Observation to Refined Strategic Issue

With the early advent of the internet, many physicians began talking about the affect it was having on patient expectations. Everyone agreed it was transforming the doctor-patient relationship, but the consequences seemed to be noisy. Doctors had less influence over what their patients were thinking, and they had to work harder to respond to the torrent of patient questions that emanated from the information they now had at their command, much of which was itself questionable.

A trend of this type certainly needs some detailed prose to describe it sufficiently. However, in the end, the trend was vetted by several groups and captured in a cause-and-effect statement that conveyed the essence of the issue that deserved the strategic attention of this particular association:

> *Patient use of the internet to find and track clinical trials regarding their particular form of cancer* (the cause) *is changing the traditional doctor/patient relationship with respect to patient involvement in diagnostic and treatment considerations* (the effect).

Note that the statement does not recommend any actions the association should take in response to this issue. That's the job of the strategy makers, which they will get to if they agree that the issue statement is accurate and important enough to deserve a strategic response. The issue could have been framed several different ways. The process invites people to read the background text and propose framing it differently.

It's also worth noting that there should be a firewall between the issue statement and any discussion of what could or should be done about it. The number-one failure point in problem-solving is not getting everyone to arrive at the same understanding of the problem before allowing any discussion on possible solutions. Once people agree on a concise statement of the issue, then they can explore possible strategies. When you hear someone say, "That is the problem and we need to…," they're promoting a solution before there's consensus on the issue. Once that happens, the conversation gets confusing and disorganized. It lacks fitness-for-use.

As a final footnote on this example, once the members and staff of the association agreed on this specific issue statement, they launched a strategy that expanded their physicians-only website to include patients, providing them with information that addresses their documented needs, including use of the internet to acquire reliable medical information.

single-sentence statement that is carefully crafted to convey a cause-and-effect relationship between the two variables.. An example of a strategic issue that is formatted in this way comes from an association that accredits engineering programs:

*The growing demand for accreditation of engineering degree programs delivered entirely by distance learning* (cause) *brings into question the site-specific requirements of the laboratory experience* (effect).

Some people confuse an issue with a topic, which has only one variable. They often assume the topic is hot enough for everyone to understand why it must be addressed, so they plow right into the action they think should be taken. This is a dangerous assumption that leads to misunderstandings. Everyone should have the same understanding of an issue and a shared sense of its significance before talking about steps that should be take to address it. It's important to note that a strategic issue provides no hint of what should be done. That comes with the strategy. The issue itself provides a clear declaration of the reason to act.

There are more strategic issues in the association's environment than any group of leaders can deal with collectively, so a sorting process develops that comes in the form of a radar screen. It imposes an arbitrary limitation on the number of issues that will be considered at any point in time. That limit is about 12 to 15.

A broad spectrum of members and other affected parties should be involved in the identification of issues that will compete for a position on the radar screen. This process can include focus groups, cafe conversations, town hall meetings, surveys, committee input, and more. In the end, the issues that qualify for the radar screen will do so based on two criteria. It will include the issues that (1) will have the greatest impact on the membership and (2) are within the association's ability to act upon effectively.

## Issues Can Be Classified by Clarity and Importance

The issues that do make it onto the radar screen will fall into several categories based on their clarity and importance. Typically this involves three groups. The first category of issues will require additional research to understand them more clearly or resolve disagreements on their importance. These issues are referred to the appropriate committee or task force for research.

In the second category are those issues that are clear enough but not urgent or high enough on the importance ranking to justify action at the current time. They are, however, on the radar screen because they warrant monitoring for possible action in the future. As a matter of course, program managers may be asked if and how they may address some aspect of these issues. The collective response will probably not amount to a succinct strategy, but the association staff is very likely addressing elements of the issue, which should be encouraged and tracked.

The third category includes those issues that are ready for prime time. These top-priority issues are candidates for strategy making. Everyone is invited to participate in the discussions that identify issues and consider their relative importance, but ultimately the board sets the priorities. This is an extension of the board's fiduciary responsibility because these strategies typically require a significant resource investment and are apt to alter the association's fundamental value propositions.

One of the more useful features of a strategic issue that is formatted as a cause-and-effect statement can be found in the utility it offers when it comes time to explore the strategy options available to the planners. There are only three. Here they are in order of their desirability, but reverse order of probability.

- **Option One:** Make the cause go away, so you don't have to worry about the consequences.

- **Option Two:** Acknowledge that the cause is not going away, so find ways to alleviate the consequences.

- **Option Three:** Acknowledge that the cause and the consequences are coming inevitably, so adapt. Become different in ways that avoid negative consequences and capitalize on the new order of things.

For example, when the Clinton administration initiated discussions about healthcare reform in 1993, coalitions formed to successfully terminate the cause. When the Obama administration took on the cause again in 2009, the same coalitions tried the same strategy but failed to appreciate the importance of both houses of Congress being aligned with the White House. Many still fought the cause to the bitter end (Option One), while others saw the writing on the wall and began working their own deals to reduce the consequences (Option 2). However, most began work on significant adaptations in the way they do business (Option 3).

The value of the three-option framework is itself threefold. It forces people to agree on the need to act before they consider possible actions. If they don't agree on the motive, they're not apt to agree on a strategy. Second, it provides an analytical format to explore a full spectrum of strategic options. Finally, it provides scanning outputs that have fitness-for-use as strategy inputs.

As more and more association members are exposed to environmental scanning systems in their work environments, they'll expect their associations to pursue environmental scanning as well. What may be more important is the fact that a good environmental scanning system in the association should provide a valued information source for their scanning efforts. This will make scanning both an administrative tool for the association and a service to the members.

## Strategy Has Four Elements

A strategy consists of four basic parts that work in sync to achieve a desired outcome. When a strategy is developed in a way that accounts for these parts in a clear and consistent manner, it offers three advantages:

- The people who are called upon to make the strategy do so more expediently because they have the same understanding of the parts that go into it and the way it works.

- The people who authorize strategies and monitor them to make sure they stay on course can do so more clearly because there is consistency in format, which is important when there are multiple strategies to evaluate and track.

- When a strategy goes astray, and they all do on occasion, the analysis to determine what's wrong is simplified by a structural invariability. One of the four parts is providing misinformation that's throwing everything off.

The four parts of a strategy include:

1. **The strategic issue.** In constructing a strategy, you start with the strategic issue, which provides a succinct statement of the motive to act. It provides a clear focal point of agreement on the force that is driving the strategy and the matter that will be resolved if the strategy succeeds. An adage from baseball is relevant here. *Keep your eye on the ball.* In this case, the issue is the ball, and the three remaining elements constitute the caliber of your swing.

2. **Desired outcomes.** The second part defines the endgame that will be achieved. These can be expressed in short, crisp statements that provide clear images of what will be accomplished if the strategy is successful. Well-crafted outcome statements are measurable and give the strategy its performance metrics.

3. **Guiding principles.** The third part sets boundaries on the strategy manager's prerogatives and introduces a critical relationship between those who approve the strategy and those who manage it. Boards approve strategies and turn the management of them over to the staff, a committee, or a task force created exclusively for that purpose. For the strategy to be intelligent, that is, to learn as it goes, managers must be free to make adjustments in real time. Nevertheless, the board has ultimate responsibility for changes that alter the outcomes. Guiding principles make cautionary statements on pitfalls that should be avoided and policies that could be affected. However, they should not be prescriptive to a point where they dictate how the outcomes will be achieved.

4. **Event sequence.** The fourth element is the action plan that defines the tasks necessary to achieve the outcomes in a manner that respects the principles. Quinn's use of the term "event sequence" rather than action plan is intended to make several important points.

## Sample Event Sequence

An association had a desired outcome that would diversify its membership by attracting a new demographic group that was emerging as a result of a new technology that affected their members. The event sequence that would make this happen was summarized as follows:

1. Develop a database of a thousand prospects from this new group.

2. Send complimentary copies of the magazine to them for three months prior to the annual meeting and include feature stories on the issues they care about.

3. Schedule several annual meeting sessions that address these issues and highlight them in the magazine issues they receive before the meeting.

4. Send customized marketing appeals to persuade them to attend the meeting.

5. Initiate a membership marketing campaign once the complimentary subscription and annual meeting tactics play out.

6. Assess the effectiveness of the effort and propose broader scale, phase-two initiatives and/or more market research to quantify their needs more accurately.

Those who manage this strategy will require much more detailed task information to make these thrusts happen. Still, from the perspective of those who approve the strategy, it provides a sketch for them to determine the viability.

---

Action plans can include any number of steps that can get increasingly micro. For Quinn, an event sequence includes four to seven major thrusts that must be completed to get from the current state described in the issue to the preferred state accounted for in the desired outcomes. The primary purpose of this very frugal expression is to show viability. It answers one simple question. Is the assertion that you can get there credible?

The four parts of strategy provide structure for analysis when a strategy goes astray as illustrated by these possibilities:

- Articulation of the issue driving the strategy was inaccurate, or like a rapidly changing virus, it morphed significantly since the strategy launch.
- One (or more) of the desired outcomes was unrealistic.
- The guiding principles were too restrictive, or they failed to anticipate the prospect of undesired outcomes.
- One of the thrusts in the event sequence was overly ambitious and/or under-funded.

The need for dialogue between a board that approves a strategy and the managers responsible for its execution is structured around the interactive nature of these four elements. This as an element of strategy making will vary according to the cultural norms of the association. As a rule of thumb, the board has the final say on the importance and characterization of the issues on the radar screen, but all are invited into the process that identifies and refines them. The outcome statements must be approved by the board, but they should ask the managers to draft them as a part of their initial work in developing the strategy sketch.

This will drive a dialogue that will make sure both parties understand each other and agree on where the strategy is bound. The principles are the exclusive domain of the board because they place boundaries on the prerogatives of the managers. The event sequence should be the exclusive domain of the managers, but it must pass the tests for viability and affordability, which the board is responsible for in the final decision to authorize a strategy.

This four-part sketch should fit on a single piece of paper and be used to keep the board informed on progress over time. The strategy sketch is available at every board meeting and updated as necessary. Some updates require board approval; others do not. The association should set its own guidelines on this. Board approval would be required if the event sequence was altered in a way that requires additional resources. However, if a more expedient way of achieving the outcomes was identified that did not affect the budget, the strategy managers should be free to make those changes and simply inform the board that the plan was revised.

As strategic planning sheds its rigid, elaborate, and somewhat imperial procedures to become a fast-moving way of maintaining conversations on the future and launching initiatives to sustain the organization, a simpler set of procedures is needed. This framework is intended to serve that purpose. Regardless of what you wind up calling it, associations must maintain stability, but adapt quickly, and have a clearly documented process to manage these opposite but complementary requirements.

# Case Studies

# A New Scan Plan

## Oncology Nursing Society
*PITTSBURGH*

**Mission:** To promote excellence in oncology nursing and quality cancer care

**Membership:** 37,000 registered nurses

**Objective:** Revise the society's scanning process to increase frequency and relevance

*"Find a process that works and stick to it."*

– Michelle Dietz, executive director, external relations and business development

### Background

ONS totally revised its scanning process beginning in 2007. In the old process, the organization did a strategic plan with the board every three years; an elaborate environmental scan and comprehensive survey would be part of that process. The comprehensive survey would ask the membership what was going on in the nursing environment. ONS staff would then produce a report on the survey results and their scanning activities, this would be published, and the board would digest the document and revise the organization's strategic plan to reflect any new trends.

Staff and the board had already been in discussion that things were changing too rapidly in the profession to put off scanning to every three years. Then Michelle Dietz, ONS executive director, external relations and business development, participated in the healthcare town hall trends meeting hosted by ASAE and led by the consultant for the *Designing Your Future* project. That experience solidified her thinking that ONS had to revise its scanning process. Her attendance at the town hall meeting was transformational; she was convinced that ONS had to do trending continuously.

## Results

Now ONS does a continual scan of the nursing environment. This comes in the form of continual feedback from the membership as well as ongoing monitoring of trade publications and government reports. Some reports of particular value are those from the Institute of Medicine and materials from the American Nursing Association.

Members provide feedback by calling in, e-mailing, and responding to mini-surveys asking what issues they see emerging in their field. ONS also conducts less frequent but more comprehensive surveys. In 2010 ONS conducted a futures survey that was very comprehensive and again asked for issues of concern in the future. From those answers, the top few responses were incorporated into a more in depth survey to further whittle down those issues for relevance.

Ongoing scanning of the media falls to the PR team, which continuously monitors and stays in touch with the media. They also pay attention to social media. They have virtual communities on Facebook, Twitter, and LinkedIn. There are staff members in the society's communications department that are dedicated to monitoring its virtual communities. They are still working on how to make this process more effective and also how to measure the success of their virtual communities.

Every year in anticipation of the annual board meeting in January, all departments pull together their analyses of what trends are emerging in each area. What is emerging as the future for nursing in general and in oncology nursing in particular? In addition to the staff they also reach out to their 30 special interest areas within the membership and ask them for the top three to five issues of concern to members. The areas of concurrence are compiled into a briefing packet for the board to review prior to the meeting. The board discusses the material in the packet to identify the trends that require action and then craft a strategy to address the specific trends.

However, they don't necessarily wait for the annual board meeting to do this. The staff is continually searching for what is new in nursing, medicine, and healthcare. If something happens through the year that the staff feels is of importance, they will again assemble a packet for discussion among the board members.

One example of a trend identified through this process was an emerging problem in the publications and education areas of ONS. Volunteers were not meeting their deadlines. This was having an adverse impact upon the organization. In publications, they were projecting revenue from anticipated books. The writers weren't meeting their deadlines; the books weren't published and for sale when scheduled. They projected revenue from those anticipated books in the budget, so the bottom line was adversely affected. Staff took this issue to the board. As a result, the board instituted policies making it easier to relieve volunteers of their responsibilities when they weren't meeting their targets. The board got behind this, and they support the staff when they enforce the policies.

### Next Steps

When ONS revised its strategic plan in 2011, the big topic of discussion was how do we define success? The big issues recently have been quality of care, electronic health records, health care reform legislation, and the Future of Nursing Report from the Institute of Medicine. ONS staff members look at these areas as they relate to their membership. What models for delivering care are developing? What are the emerging trends in nursing care?

Staff have data from their surveys and from their scanning activities, but they also track their members' and non-members' usage of their programs and publications. In addition, they have a huge store of data of non-members who have completed a certification process to become "chemo cardholders," so they know they have relevance for a much larger community than just their members. They are working to develop a robust data warehousing system so that they can process these numbers more efficiently.

ONS is still searching for the best methods to get information out to its members about the emerging trends in their profession. Members receive e-mail blasts, but they complain about getting too many messages. The ONS website is segmented based on the content that would be of most interest to specific people. Each of the society's special interest groups has a separate section on the website, so staff will post specific information to those sections. They have established virtual communities on the site as well.

Overall, their processes for conducting the scans are working well, but Dietz and other staff are always thinking about how to stay focused on the future.

CASE STUDY 2

# *Tracking Trends*

## American Dental Association
*CHICAGO*

**Mission:** Foster the success of a diverse membership and advance the oral health of the public

**Membership:** 150,000+

**Objective:** Establish a defined framework for scanning

> *"Follow what is happening in your profession and then be ready for it. Don't wait; act."*
> – Dr. Al Guay, chief policy officer

### Background

The American Dental Association conducts a formal environmental scan twice a year. The organization adopted this formal framework for scanning in 2006. Staff members with responsibilities in six focus areas track information on trends that could affect the dentistry profession: education, government and public relations, communications, health policy, membership, and dental practice.

Their information comes from a variety of sources, including mass media, social media, government reports, conferences, member feedback (through calls and meetings), online searches, and other sources. Staff assembles this information into a 130-plus-page document, which is sent to ADA's strategic planning committee for review.

The committee discusses the information as far as its implications for the practice of dentistry and then makes recommendations to the board of trustees. In total it takes about four years for the ADA to adopt a policy. The board has to debate it and further research it. Then the membership has to vote on it. It is a very top-down process.

## Results

Dr. Al Guay, ADA's chief policy officer, contributes to the section of the environmental scan document devoted to dental practice. Guay has 26 years of experience as an orthodontist as well as 19 years of experience at the ADA, 10 years as its chief policy officer. From his perspective, having a defined scan process has improved the ADA's scan results.

His experience indicates that what happens in health care happens in dentistry several years later, so he closely tracks what is happening in the medical field. He has also found that new trends in healthcare tend to start on the west coast and travel east, so he pays close attention to what is happening in medicine on the west coast.

What's good about this approach is that new ideas and modalities in medicine tend to be proven or discredited by the time they filter down to dentistry. When it does reach their profession, he can say, "that's been discredited, or that's been proven."

To stay informed, Guay reads numerous publications to see what's coming next for ADA and its members. He regularly reads information from foundations to see what medical research they are funding. He also monitors publications from medical organizations and the federal government, again with a focus on what kinds of projects are receiving funding. Every day, in addition to the dental press, he reads *The New York Times* and *The Wall Street Journal. Health Affairs,* the *Journal of the American Medical Association,* and the *Harvard Business Review* are also among the key publications that he reads regularly.

In addition, Guay finds attendance at conferences very productive because of the likelihood that he'll be introduced to new ideas, pilot programs, and contacts. For instance, he has attended the Pay for Performance Summit in California every year since its inception and was able to track the development of this trend over several years. When this trend first emerged in medicine, his colleagues in dentistry dismissed it as unlikely to affect their field. He persisted in his belief that this trend would in fact affect dentistry and worked with the board to develop a policy. Now, as pay for performance make its way into dentistry, the ADA is ready with its policy.

Another emerging trend that Guay identified was commons-based peer production, which also started in medicine. He saw this as a threat to dentistry right away. ADA counts on revenue from its proprietary information, and this new Wikipedia model of information-sharing posed a threat to this revenue. Many colleagues in dentistry discounted this trend. Now it is here, and dentists are really threatened.

The threat is two-pronged. First, much of the ADA's information, especially related to professional knowledge and dental practice information on the ADA website, had previously been secured behind firewalls and required a password (obtained through membership dues) to gain access, but the trend and expectation on the internet is away from proprietary information and more to common-source information. Likewise, dentists in practice are struggling to keep information they have written and posted on their websites proprietary. The ADA hasn't adopted a policy on this issue, but is adapting internal activities and budgetary structures to reflect the new reality and also advising dentists to adapt their thinking related to proprietary information.

According to Guay, "environmental scanning is absolutely critical in a rapidly changing world. Too often associations react to new trends when it's too late. The best time to influence the direction that new trends take is in the early days, while the issue is still being shaped."

However, he thinks that a lot of people engaging in scanning aren't grounded in useful reality. In the past, ADA hired a couple of consultants to conduct scans for them, and the information wasn't really useful. For example, one of the futurists predicted that airplane bodies would be made of transparent plastic and passengers and crew would be able to look out of the airplane in any direction. Now, of what use is that to dentistry?

# And the Survey Says...

## Credit Union National Association

*WASHINGTON, DC*

**Mission:** CUNA supports, protects, unifies, and advances the credit union movement

**Membership:** 6,500+ state and federally chartered credit unions

**Objective:** To monitor trends and develop scanning tools for members

> *"Associations that want to get into environmental scanning should start by doing a survey of their members to find out what their concerns and needs are, and then focus on addressing the most pressing needs first. From there you can add and enhance."*
> **– Steve Rodgers, editorial director**

### Background

The Credit Union National Association (CUNA) does continuous, extensive environmental scanning on many fronts: economic environment, business environment and behavior, and the political/legislative environment. CUNA's *E-Scan Report* is updated annually and assembled into several products to help the organization's member credit unions stay current with trends and facilitate their strategic planning efforts. These products include a subscription to an e-scan newsletter and a *Strategic Planning Guide.* The results of CUNA's environmental scanning also inform the decisions of the national board of directors and are distributed to them through the *E-Scan Report,* briefing booklets, and action papers.

The CUNA board of directors goes through a strategic planning process annually. All of the board members are also CEOs or senior managers of credit unions, so they know what is going on in their local areas and benefit from receiving the *E-Scan Report.* CUNA brings in a facilitator to help the board through the strategic planning process. The facilitator also provides information about trends, especially market data. The board goes through a SWOT analysis and engages in a discussion about which trends are likely important.

The national board's strategic plan is officially a three-year plan even though it is reviewed annually. The strategic planning session is held in June every year. The staff members then evaluate the plan to see what internal adjustments need to be made in response to new trends, if any. Any budgetary ramifications are addressed in a September planning session. The new plan goes into effect in January and is again reviewed in June.

CUNA staff members by and large do not interact with the national board during the national board's strategic planning process. Other than access to the *E-Scan Report,* the national board doesn't get briefings from CUNA staff experts prior to their meetings.

While staff members do not interact directly with board members, they are empowered to address important trends as they encounter them. For instance, the subject of social media is covered in the marketing chapter of CUNA's *E-Scan Report.* Generally, the chapter discusses its importance to credit unions in terms of protecting their brands and marketing their products and services.

Younger staff members kept saying that credit unions were being discussed on social media sites and that CUNA needed to get involved. The younger staff members were empowered to join in these discussions and create official CUNA social media groups.

In most cases, internal research, primarily conducted using surveys, serves as CUNA's barometer for scanning and addressing issues important to its members. For instance, during the course of a year, the magazine's editorial team might conduct 30 surveys. Most are mini-surveys, but some contain 100 or more questions that ask member/subscriber respondents to rate the importance of issues and their relevance to them. A reliable indicator of the relevance of articles in the magazine is how much feedback an article generates.

CUNA has an editorial board made up of members, who look out for what is going on in their local areas. The editorial board will recommend articles, and then the communications department will research the issues with the help of the CUNA research department and possibly conduct a mini-survey. If the topic rises to the level of significant interest, a journalist will be assigned to write the article.

Occasionally there will be bigger issues that would warrant the publication of a dedicated research report. CUNA's research department would conduct a survey of the members and analyze the results. The organization judges the relevance of the issue to members through sales of the report. Two examples would be a report on credit union fees and one on prompt corrective action.

CUNA is primarily an advocacy group, and the organization conducts a survey of voters every year. A random sample of 1,000 voters is contacted by telephone and asked to respond to 60–70 questions. Some questions get asked every year, but some are new to the survey in response to new issues. In addition to CUNA's national survey, the association's regional and state offices also do regular surveys. They often coordinate their surveying efforts, so some questions are always asked. By the end of the year, they can end up with 12,000–14,000 responses to one question. With so much data, they can cross tab issues regionally and create many demographic categories.

## Results

Generally the organization has not missed many trends, but rather has spotted things that were expected to be small that turned out to be big. One trend spotted very early, in 2002 or earlier, was the bubble in the real estate market. This observation made it into the *E-Scan Report* for several years. What was missed was the magnitude of this trend. CUNA didn't expect that it was going to almost bring down the entire global banking system.

Another trend CUNA identified through scanning was the rise in consumer debt. In the 80s, consumer debt averaged two thirds of take-home pay. In the 90s, it kept rising, and this ominous trend was highlighted in the *E-Scan Report*. In the 2000s, consumer debt was up to 130 percent of take-home pay, which obviously had disastrous results.

A third trend spotted was the explosion of technology and its quick adoption by consumers. It was only a few years prior that debit cards came out, and now people can do all their banking on the computer or smartphone. This has had a tremendous impact on credit union operations.

Another trend that CUNA's research department spotted through Census Bureau reports was the growth of the immigrant population in the United States, which has tremendous implications for credit unions because they have to figure out ways to reach this new community.

## Next Steps

The final product of environmental scanning should be easy to distribute and should take into account the volatile nature of the information. CUNA has developed strategic planning tools for credit unions, which are for sale on the association's website. Strategic planning is absolutely essential for credit unions to have a hope of anticipating the future. There is a science to survey research, economic forecasting, and advocacy. It's important to have a plan and stick to it, but associations have to know when to push and when to let up. It doesn't pay to be too far out in front of certain issues.

# All Together Now: Scanning and Strategic Planning

## Napa Valley Vintners

*ST. HELENA, CALIFORNIA*

**Membership:** 430 wineries in the Napa Valley

**Mission:** To protect the Napa Valley appellation against incursion and keep the brand strong

**Objective:** To monitor issues

> *"Find out what members want and need. Craft your communications with the purpose of fulfilling that need. Also, be inclusive. Give credit where it's due and give it often. It is very important that the board be inclusive."*
> – Terry Hall, director of communications

### Background

Napa Valley Vintners (NVV) works with federal, state, and world officials to protect the brand. Any issue that threatens to impede or hinder their members' ability to market their wines is a threat. Environmental, agricultural, and cultural issues all could have an impact.

NVV maintains relationships with a lot of industry partners to help the organization respond to issues and has a lot of interaction with its members. NVV's members are always coming to staff with their issues, both by telephone and at their meetings and programs.

NVV uses Zoomerang to conduct mini-surveys to track the relevance of issues. It is a very good platform that allows NVV to keep surveys simple and short. That's very important because most of the organization's members are small businesses, and the owners are very busy. Staff will compile a list of issues they've heard of recently and ask members whether they are a concern for them. Staff will then compile these results and present them to NVV's business practices committee. The committee members discuss emerging issues among themselves and also at town hall meetings among vintners in different areas of the valley.

If the need arises, NVV will conduct a symposium about a very weighty topic, and the organization will work with other advocacy groups to further its cause. One weighty topic was the discovery of the European grapevine moth in the valley. This pest has caused great disruption and economic hardship among vintners. Once the moths were discovered in traps, NVV reached out to partners across the globe to find the best practices for dealing with the moth and then held symposia for members to educate them on those best practices.

NVV has a very robust website as well as groups on Facebook and Yahoo. A member relations manager on NVV's staff of 23 has the specific duty of monitoring the groups and tweets. NVV produces an annual and semi-annual report but does most of its communicating through the website.

Committees report to NVV's board of 11 members. The board then takes action. Board members are very active in environmental scanning. They are all vintners in the community, so they're hearing from people and other vintners about emerging issues all the time. In addition each board member is active on at least one committee, so they're getting feedback on issues in this way as well. Committees also have non-vintner community leaders as members.

### Results
Issues identified by members definitely affect the organization's strategic planning process, which takes place every three years. It begins with a very defined and outlined process for gathering information to be included in the strategic planning briefing booklet:

- Staff pulls together the old strategic plan, which is centered on NVV's mission, vision, and goals. Each of these three areas will have measures for success in each of the three years of the plan; for the mission area, there will be assigned tactics for years one, two, and three. At the end of each year staff and the board will evaluate whether they met their goals for the year and make adjustments if necessary or pledge to redouble efforts.

- Staff members are also responsible for pulling together information from industry partners, state officials and agencies, feedback from customers and the local community, and other sources.

- Napa Valley Vintners has a number of standing committees that brainstorm for ideas on the mission, vision, and goals of the organization. These ideas are discussed, prioritized, and sent to the board.

- Board members attend neighborhood meetings, which bring together vintners in the far corners of the valley for town hall meetings. Information flows back and forth. Staff members take notes on issues, concerns, and ideas.

- In addition the membership receives a survey which asks them to rate programs and performance on goals. These results provide more metrics to consider in the planning process.

Just prior to the beginning of the strategic planning process, the staff and board each participate in separate retreats to strategize on tactics and reacquaint themselves with the existing strategic plan and the measures for progress on each of them. Part of every strategic planning process is to assess progress on the measures for success.

The board then meets to discuss the issues that have been presented in the packet, weigh new issues against old issues, and discuss whether the mission, vision, and goals of the organization need recalibration, refinement, or redefinition. Once the board has agreed on a new strategic plan, it is sent to NVV members, who have an opportunity to comment on the new strategic plan. The board will consider comments and adjust the plan if necessary. Once the plan clears this step, it is published.

The next steps are to build the budget to support the strategic plan and develop tactics for moving forward. NVV has had this same strategic planning process for the past 15 years, which covers five strategic plans. This current process replaced a very hit or miss process and was largely the work of their executive director, Linda Reiff, who arrived at NVV 15 years ago.

The strategic plan is very useful in keeping everyone focused. Industry partners or others are constantly coming to NVV asking for support (and staff resources) of new initiatives. Staff and the board are able to weigh these requests against the mission, vision, and goals in the strategic plan to assess whether the new initiative will complement or distract from the strategic plan.

There are always issues arising. For example, interstate shipping is a new one. NVV worked with the state agricultural board to smooth out barriers to being able to do this. Some states forbid it, or some counties, and then there are global concerns around this issue as well.

Staff members are in continuous communication with members, who are all Napa Valley vintners. NVV issues a very short daily blast to members that highlights one issue or topic and provides a link back to the website if someone wants to read more about it. The daily blast could be an industry issue, a regulatory issue, an announcement of an upcoming speaker at one of NVV's meetings, or the results of one of their mini-surveys.

**Next Steps**

- Continue to establish NVV as the go-to resource for information by benchmarking and working hard to establish two-way communication between and among members.
- Work with the board and staff to engender a collaborative environment.
- Make sure volunteers know how valuable and appreciated they are.

# Asked and Answered

## Georgia Society of Association Executives
*ATLANTA*

**Membership:** Full-time professionals of voluntary, trade, professional, philanthropic, technical or similar organizations

**Mission:** To advance the profession of association management and to enhance the professionalism of association executives

**Objective:** To identify and track the issues facing members

> *"Make time to do environmental scanning. It is easy to get caught up in the day-to-day minutiae of the job, but you can't ignore innovation and scanning. You have to build it into your schedule. You just have to."*
> – Wendy W. Kavanaugh, CAE, president

### Background

The basis of GSAE's environmental scanning is to ask a lot of questions of the members, both in person and on the phone. The organization regularly conducts mini-surveys of the membership asking, what keeps you up at night? What challenges are you facing?

Atlanta in particular and Georgia overall had been heavily invested in the booming housing and construction market for a long time, so the economic downturn has really hit hard. People are struggling, especially in the financial services industry. GSAE's members have shared how they're struggling to stay ahead in this environment. This is one area where the mini-surveys have helped a lot.

GSAE has three membership committees that look specifically at new, mid-career, and retiring association executives, again asking them in surveys what keeps them up at night? These activities really drive their professional development schedule. GSAE went through a process to reach out to potential members and non-members to ask if there were issues with GSAE's brand identity and marketing activities. Survey results reassured them the

GSAE brand is very strong in Georgia. This was especially reassuring to the board, and the association has taken on projects and activities that will hopefully attract members earlier in their careers.

GSAE has four quarterly luncheons for members and an annual meeting. The association's two staff members are both engaged in environmental scanning and present survey findings to members at those meetings as well as use them to take the pulse of members. Internally they do their own electronic keyword searches to stay ahead. Also, their members will call them and ask them to do keyword searches on their behalf, which helps them stay ahead.

Wendy Kavanaugh, the association's president, has been at GSAE since 2005, and she's been doing scanning since then. Her predecessor also did significant scanning, so the organization has been doing scanning for a long time. It's institutionalized at this point. GSAE's members are used to responding to surveys and participating in focus groups. New tools, such as Zoomerang and Survey Monkey, have made it much easier to conduct mini-surveys and that has helped with the collection process.

GSAE board members are doing their own scanning for their associations, or asking Kavanaugh to do it for them. They do SWOT analyses at board retreats in preparation for their strategic plan updates. They used to update the strategic plan every five years, but now it is on a two- to three-year cycle. The board discusses trends and scanning activities every 18 months.

### Results

GSAE's strategic planning process begins with data. The association always asks satisfaction questions on surveys to get a reading on which programs are working and which ones have lost their edge. Through this process, GSAE developed its Leadership Academy. Leadership and management realized from surveying and talking to colleagues in Georgia and Atlanta that there was a void in this area and that GSAE had the expertise to fill that void.

GSAE's board is not risk averse, but the members do like to have some data to support their decisions. They occasionally bring in outside contractors to lead their strategic planning updates. If so, the contractor will want to ask specific questions on a survey to use the results. However, GSAE always asks variations of the same questions about how valuable their offerings are and how good they are doing at meeting members' needs. GSAE leadership and management believes in modeling best practices and asks, what's important to you? They take pulse surveys.

Kavanaugh feels it is also very important to talk to leaders and members because written surveys can be too static. GSAE also hosts occasional focus groups to talk about the direction the association is headed. The focus groups and conversations are a great way to hone in on what's working and not working. GSAE has to focus its resources and manage expectations. The association has only a two-person staff, so they want to be sure they're being their most productive on programs and activities that add value to the members.

GSAE is fortunate in that volunteers do a lot of work. GSAE is able to track satisfaction with programs, and if two years pass without progress on a goal or project, staff and volunteers go back and reevaluate.

Because of the small staff, GSAE relies on volunteers to stay up with social media sites. Some members are really into social media and will provide summaries of what's being said on sites to members and staff. This is working out well.

Another resource GSAE frequently taps is the network of other state societies of association executives around the country. A colleague at the Florida SAE told Wendy about *Race for Relevance* by Harrison Coerver and Mary Byers, CAE. She distributed that information to her members, and the response was fantastic. They sold 50 books and drew big crowds at discussions related to the book. This was an example of how you have to respond quickly and be nimble to stay relevant.

GSAE has found that it has the best luck with requests for assistance from volunteers by communicating a lot. Identify a need, look for a good candidate, and engage him or her. A lot of the needs are identified in the strategic planning process when the association asks where we are and what we need to be doing. Staff are very specific in their asks. It's important to share ownership. They do the plan, identify activities and work that needs to be done, and go in search of volunteers.

### Next Steps

Kavanaugh tracks what BoardSource is doing because she finds the organization to be a good resource. Smith Bucklin's alert newsletter also is a good resource. She is aware of the ASAE Trends database and recently visited it. She finds it a very valuable resource and encourages her members to use it. She is aware of all of the ASAE futures publications and thinks they are good references for people starting out with environmental scanning.

# Extra! Extra! Read All About It

## Global Cold Chain Alliance

*ALEXANDRIA, VIRGINIA*

**Membership:** 345 public refrigerated warehouse companies, 1,012 facilities, 80 construction companies, 112 transportation companies, and 387 suppliers to the industry

**Mission:** Unite partners to be innovative leaders in the temperature-controlled products industry

**Objective:** Identify and monitor trends on an international scale

> *"Unless you're a statistician or an economist, partner with someone with that expertise if you are about to start scanning because the data can be overwhelming. Look for potential partners."*
> – Tori Liu, director, marketing and communications

### Background

Formed in 2007, The Global Cold Chain Alliance (GCCA) is an international alliance of four separate associations, all concerned with the storage and transportation of food products. GCCA is still finding its way as far as establishing a global presence, but the organization has personnel and offices in Europe, Latin America, China, and India. The organization needed a presence in those regions to attract and service members; members wanted programs, meetings, and events specifically targeted to those regions.

Given GCCA's scope, staff members spend a great amount of time and effort in keeping up with news about the industry. The alliance has members in 65 countries, so it can be challenging. They read their trade press; for example, the *Quick Frozen Food Journal* is one very helpful publication. The USDA has been collecting data on cold storage facilities in the U.S. since WWII, and its publication is very helpful as well. Occasionally there will be articles about cold storage in the mass media, but not very often. They have set up a Google weekly scan of mass media to look for those.

The alliance conducts two very comprehensive surveys biennially. GCCA's product and benchmarking study compiles data on performance indicators worldwide and looks at everything from human resources to operational performance. The alliance sells the report, and it is much anticipated in the industry.

GCCA's other study is a capacity report that studies the industry's infrastructure worldwide: warehouses, ports, airports, both existing and under planning, and development. This is a very challenging report to produce in that most of the new activity is going on in newer markets with less ability to communicate about their activities. They work with embassies and the trade press to find out what is going on. They view this as an opportunity to educate some of the newer players to the alliance and also to establish best practices. The alliance also sells this report, but the information that is contained in it also gets much broader dissemination through GCCA's magazine and other information sources. These surveys and reports have been produced since the 1990s.

GCCA is not a leader in social media but is involved. The alliance has groups on LinkedIn and Facebook and has people looking in daily to see what's being said there. They will often see a discussion about a specific issue or topic break out, and this will lead to an article in their newsletter. There might be a spike in electronic conversation about worker safety and OSHA, for example. Alliance staff members, however, have to be mindful that other parts of the world don't want a newsletter full of news from the United States. They are seeing that folks in Asia, especially India and other emerging countries, ask a lot of questions through the LinkedIn group.

The alliance uses e-newsletters to aggregate information learned through other publications and to get it out to their members. E-newsletters are produced weekly, bimonthly, and monthly for the different organization members in their alliance. GCCA's larger magazine is published every other month. GCCA is in the process of revamping its website to make it more interactive and possibly replace some of the e-newsletters. Staff envision that the alliance will be more involved in social media with Twitter and news feeds once that process is completed.

GCCA board members are involved in environmental scanning. The board is international, and board members watch what is going on in their parts of the world as far as new infrastructure projects and resources devoted to the cold chain. Since GCCA has four different boards representing the four organizations, it is a very large board, so they rely on their trends and association program committees to discuss emerging issues. They also have a past chairman's council that they convene every other year specifically to consider emerging issues.

The alliance conducts a quarterly survey of the board that is focused on the financial performance of the separate industries. These surveys are helpful in spotting trends. The board has also started having a roundtable discussion of trends and issues at board meetings, and this has been very well received by the board; participation has been spirited and the feedback they've gotten from the board has been very positive.

Members are frequently in contact with the alliance, offering issues of concern. There was a sense among the staff that they weren't using this information well, so they have recently implemented a new association management system, which enables them to capture conversations between staff and members. The new software enables them to do a query to see what words are turning up most frequently in conversation. They've instituted a new feature in their staff meetings where people share what they've heard recently from members.

### Results

One trend GCCA has spotted is the increased integration of the industry. Some of the warehouse members were starting trucking operations and some of the logistics members were building warehouses. Staff and leadership predicted that this was a trend that would continue, and that has proven to be the case. How did they notice this? They gathered feedback from their members, who were talking about how they were branching out. Then, they saw members' press releases about new facilities and new services. They have modified GCCA surveys to capture this information.

# Staff-Driven Scanning

## National Ground Water Association
### WESTERVILLE, OHIO

**Membership:** U.S. and international groundwater professionals—
contractors, scientists and engineers, equipment
manufacturers, and suppliers

**Mission:** Dedicated to advancing groundwater knowledge

**Objective:** Encourage members to be more involved in discussions
about the future of their industry

*"Try different ways of articulating the issues to engage the
membership. Keep putting the information in front of the members
in different ways. Then, when you do gain some traction on a
discussion and come up with issues, put them out there and let the
marketplace decide if you've got it right. Keep it simple. Volunteers
often won't have your experience and perspective. You have to
empathize with them and share their concerns."*
– Kevin B. McCray, CAE, chief executive officer

### Background

NGWA has a very diverse membership that includes very large multinational corporations and small business owners whose work is normally
close to their home location. It is an ongoing challenge for members to
understand the concerns of the other group and for the staff to think about
these different demographics and members' concerns. Both populations
are represented on the association's board. Staff members persevere by
presenting the issues and challenges in different ways using different
terminology to meet this challenge.

NGWA's environmental scanning relies on what the staff can see and
communicate to the board. NGWA CEO Kevin B. McCray, CAE, constantly
reads the available literature from the water and environmental sectors. He
also pays attention to small business trends. He monitors a number of ASAE
online communities, journals, and educational events on topics of interest

whenever he can fit them in. He attends a lot of events locally and listens to what his peers say about their concerns. He regularly reads *Wired, Popular Science,* and the *Economist* to look for trends outside the water environment.

McCray recently loaded a Smartphone app called ZITE, an aggregator of information related to the topics he chose. NGWA subscribes to Melt Water, an aggregator of online sources related to water and the environment. He is constantly on the lookout for good tools that can help him keep up with all the information that floods in.

Most of his members are struggling to stay alive in a very tough economic environment. They don't feel like they have the time to give to a discussion about potential issues, even though they want to know what is coming on the horizon. He has this same challenge at times with his board. He has to guard against being out in front of an issue when he's really not sure if it will pan out. To get board members thinking about the future, he provides little snippets of information about issues he's spotted in monthly updates for his board: the issue and its strategic implications. He expects them to read it, think about it, and discuss it with members in the field.

NGWA has more people volunteering for committees than they have slots, so he's invited those without formal committee assignments to be environmental scanners to get more people thinking about trends. The reaction has been limited, however, and there's too much reliance on staff to guide the discussion. The members are very focused on keeping their businesses going, which is getting harder and harder as the tax money to fund projects becomes less available.

### Next Steps

Even though it's sometimes difficult to get members to respond to emerging issues, McCray says association CEOs have to get out and listen to what people are talking about and be a part of the broader community. What is your member saying, and what can you do about it?

For example, he was always hearing from his members that their main gripe was that they had so much trouble pricing jobs. As a consequence, they were losing money on too many of them, so the association created a calculator on its website. Members can go there and plug in some numbers. Some costs are industry-wide, so members could see what their costs were going to be, and they could better estimate what their bids would be. This tool has been really useful.

His individual members can join task groups to respond to issues that come up. Here again he feels that this activity is staff-driven, especially in terms of issue identification. He's still trying to come up with a system that gets the members more involved in the process. He finds that he identifies most of the issues by talking to people at meetings and on the telephone in addition to monitoring listservers and reading digests.

He communicates issues to the members via NGWA's website and magazine as well as e-mail. He expects all his managers to monitor the prominent social media sites and respond where appropriate. The problem is that there are too many of them. What's needed is a way to get a digest of what's going on with all of them.

# Appendices

# Mapping Your Personal Future

Adapted from *Designing Your Future,* Appendix 7

## Objectives

This exercise is designed to help you think through your own personal future before going on to map the future of your association.

## Approach

This exercise outlines a set of nine questions designed to help you think through and map out your preferred future. The exercise can be done in one sitting and revisited regularly or conducted over a period of days, weeks, or months as you explore the changes taking place in your world and start to evolve a vision of what you want to achieve.

1. **What is my "probable almost-certain future"?** If you continue on your current career path, what will your professional, personal, and family life look like in 5 to 10 years?

2. **What is my "preferred future"?** What are your true goals? What would happen if you could maximize or go beyond your probable almost-certain future and have what you really desire? What would success look like for you in 5 to 10 years? If you succeed, what will be happening in your organizational, professional, personal, and family life?

3. **What assumptions am I making?** What assumptions are you making about the world around you, the trends that will shape it, and the factors that will be important? What key changes do you assume will occur? What do you assume will not change about

your external environment, work, family, and friends? How do the assumptions in your preferred future differ from those in your probable almost-certain future? Which negative assumptions start to disappear?

4. **Who are my future role models?** Who best display the key aspects of the future you want? Who's doing what you want to do? Who's displaying the behaviors you want to exhibit? There may be many—each doing parts well. The key is studying and practicing their behaviors.

5. **How do I make it happen?** What key steps will take you in the desired direction? What will you do in the next year, the next 6 months, the next 3 months, the next 30 days, next week, tomorrow? What comes first? Remember the vision; focus on those vital few tasks.

6. **What/who would be with me?** Which organizations, personal resources, and individuals are essential to your success? How many are already there? How can you bring in those elements that are missing in your life?

7. **What/who wouldn't be there?** What or who currently holds you back? What must you let go of? For example, which people drag you down, make you lose self-respect, or generally stop you believing in yourself and fulfilling your potential? How can you change your relationship with them in a sensitive manner or distance yourself from them?

8. **How do I make it sustainable?** How do you avoid trying to do too much too quickly, then losing momentum because you can't sustain it? How can you make the choices and changes stick? What lessons can you learn from your past successes?

9. **Who do I want as my future coach/conscience?** Who could you ask to help you do regular progress reviews against your future roadmap? Choose people who will ask questions about what you are doing to achieve the vision without judging you, exploring what is and isn't working and helping you see what you can learn from both.

# Template for Reporting on a Trend or Issue

Adapted from *Exploring the Future*

When reporting on a trend or issue, follow this format:

Person reporting: _____

Trend or issue: _____

## Information Sources Used

| List people, websites (include URLs), publications, etc., used to gather the information for this report | Rate the quality of each source (excellent, good, fair, poor) |
|---|---|
| | |

## Summary of Findings

Provide an objective overview of your findings. Provide a brief background and facts associated with the trend or issue.

_____

_____

_____

_____

_____

## Key Insights

Based on what you have learned, address the following:

**Implications/Consequences**—What are the most important implications or consequences for the association? In particular, point out opportunities or threats.

_____

_____

_____

_____

**Action Required**

_____

_____

_____

_____

**"Urgency Factor"**—What is the time frame? Is immediate action or attention required?

_____

_____

# About the Authors

**James Dalton,** president of Strategic Counsel, is a management consultant to the nonprofit community with specialties in customer research, process improvement, strategic planning, and leadership development.

**Alan Balkema** is an independent writer, consultant, and active volunteer, now semi-retired and living in Dublin, Ireland.